FROM A BURNING LEGACY OF HATE
TO AN INSPIRED CRUSADE
FOR BROTHERHOOD

The harsh lessons of Hitler's dreaded SS were
branded into young Traugott Vogel's soul.

In 1944 the Nazi youth stood before the
bombed-out ruins of his once proud home; he
vowed to seek vengeance.

With Germany's defeat, Vogel's dreams died—
and became a living nightmare. Despised, im-
poverished and consumed by hatred, his life
seemed over.

Then, a simple kindness transformed Traugott
Vogel's despair. A dramatic experience gave him
the power of faith and swept him up in the en-
nobling mission for world peace that has inspired
millions.

UNDER THE SS SHADOW
The true story of one man's courageous battle
against the terrors of his past

By Traugott Vogel
with Shirley Stephens

Under the SS Shadow

Traugott Vogel
with
Shirley Stephens

BANTAM BOOKS · TORONTO · NEW YORK · LONDON

UNDER THE SS SHADOW

*A Bantam Book / published by arrangement with
Broadman Press*

PRINTING HISTORY

*Broadman Press edition published December 1976
Bantam edition / April 1978*

*All Scripture quotations marked KJV are taken from the King
James Version of the Bible.*

*All Scripture quotations marked RSV are taken from the
Revised Standard Version of the Bible.*

*Bantam Books are published by Bantam Books, Inc. Its trade-
mark, consisting of the words "Bantam Books" and the por-
trayal of a bantam, is registered in the United States Patent
Office and in other countries. Marca Registrada. Bantam
Books, Inc., 666 Fifth Avenue, New York, New York 10019.*

PRINTED IN THE UNITED STATES OF AMERICA

Contents

Preface

"How could the German people go along with Hitler?" I asked Traugott Vogel.

"Patriotism," was his quick response. "We loved our country and wanted it to be great again," he added.

"Was that all? Did you have any other reasons?"

"Well, it was exciting and . . . I wanted to be just like my father. I wanted to wear an SS uniform. My father was my idol."

Under the SS Shadow is Traugott Vogel's story—the true story of the son of an SS officer. Traugott was inducted into the Hitler Youth at the age of ten and proudly became a part of Germany's military force at the age of fifteen. Then his dreams died with Germany's defeat. Years of struggle followed—struggle to be free of the SS label, struggle to find meaning in life, struggle to forgive the men who murdered his father.

My pastor, Bob Norman, got the ball rolling. He heard Traugott tell his story. "That's got to be a book," Bob said. I borrowed a cassette tape from Dick and Edith Franz and listened to the capsuled account of Traugott's story. I shed tears, agonized, and laughed as I listened to his experiences. I, too, said, "That's a story that *must* be shared."

In March of 1974 I flew to Midland, Texas, then went by car to Sterling City to spend a week with the Vogel family—Traugott, Holdine, and their four children: Emanuel, Michael, Dolores, Johanna. What a delightful experience! At one moment I was in a home that was thoroughly German. Then, in the next moment, they were all so American.

At the end of the week I boarded the plane for

Nashville with the story in my heart as well as my head. With great excitement I began to share Traugott Vogel's story—with you.

Shirley Stephens

Nashville, Tennessee
June, 1976

I
The Hitler Youth

I looked at the clock. 3:30 P.M. The after-school meeting of the Hitler Youth had begun thirty minutes ago. I fought back the tears. The meeting was one of the most exciting events in my life.

That morning I had awakened with a bad cold. Knowing my mother, I decided I had better start working on her early. "I'll probably feel better by this afternoon," I told her when she walked into my room to check on me.

She laughed. "Noooo, you won't." She had a way of stretching out her *o*'s. "Look at those eyes," she said, pointing a finger at me. "And you coughed all night."

I sat up in bed and looked across the narrow space into the mirror. My eyes did look terrible. They were puffy and red. And they hurt a little, too; but I didn't mention that.

"I've got to go to the Hitler Youth meeting," I begged. "Everybody goes, no matter what."

"But *you* won't go, no matter what!" she said sharply.

"I've got to. They'll come after me."

"You can't tell me that kids go when they're sick," she insisted.

"Nobody ever misses," I assured her.

"That's too bad. I'm afraid you'll have to be the first. If you had kept better care of yourself yesterday you wouldn't be so sick today. Out there bareheaded and with no jacket in this weather! Maybe you'll use your head next time."

"But Mutti (Mother), you don't know what happens when someone doesn't show up. Fred really got in trouble last week. They took him to the meeting in a police car."

"Was he sick?"

"No, but . . ."

"You're not going," she said with finality.

"Mutti, you don't understand."

"I understand that you don't go to the meeting if you don't go to school," she said firmly. "Besides, if you did all that marching and played those war games, you would be sick for a week. Missing one meeting won't kill you, anyway. You can go next time."

"But they'll come after me. They'll make me go. You've got to understand." The tears rolled down my cheeks. "Please, I've got to go," I sobbed.

She looked surprised and amused at the same time. "Oh, Traugott," she said smiling, "you are too serious." She sat down beside me and patted my leg. "Just forget about the meeting and get some rest. Then you'll get well right away." She stood up, pulled the covers over my shoulders, and leaned down to kiss me on the cheek. "You'll be all right. Don't worry," she added with unusual tenderness in her voice.

I knew it was futile to argue anymore. I couldn't change her mind. She was a stubborn mother—loving, but stubborn when her mind was made up. Still, I couldn't give up completely. Maybe I could think up a better strategy by the afternoon. I desperately wanted to go.

At lunchtime Berta, our maid, brought me some soup and a cup of hot tea with a special mixture of honey and lemon in it.

I sat up in bed and put my pillows behind my back. "I hate that hot tea," I snarled.

"Drink it," Berta said abruptly, putting the tray across my legs. "It will make you feel better."

"What good will it do? I can't go anywhere."

"Here, drink it," she insisted, as she dipped the spoon into the tea and lifted it to my mouth.

I drank it and found that it was better than I remembered.

"Berta, do you think there's any chance that I can go to the meeting?"

"You know the answer to that question. There's no chance at all. Besides, your mother is gone now. She won't be back until late this afternoon."

"But they'll come after me. You know the Führer said every boy over ten must attend the meetings of the Hitler Youth."

"I know," she said solemnly. "So young, too."

That was that. I didn't dare ask my father. He let Mutti decide about things like this.

I slept fitfully all afternoon, waking up every hour or so. The meeting was on my mind every time I woke up. I pictured my group leader, Erich Dietrich. His face was stern, never breaking into a smile. "You are Germany's future," he repeated incessantly and pompously. "You must be strong and courageous." At eleven, I was determined to get stronger and more courageous. I was going to be just like my father. He was really strong and courageous. Someday I would wear an SS uniform like his.

I looked at the clock again. 3:40 P.M. I thought of my friends at the meeting, having fun. "They're probably playing a war game right now," I whispered. "And I'm missing it. Darn! Darn! Darn!"

The sound of a car motor interrupted my thoughts. I ran to my bedroom window and pulled back the curtains in time to see a car turn in our driveway. Slowly the small car came up our long driveway. It was a familiar and foreboding sight. I had seen cars like this one many times, patrolling the streets of Augsburg. On the door was the familiar insignia of the Augsburg police. "I knew it," I gasped. "There they are. They've come after me." I looked for a place to hide. But where? They would find me. No one could elude the police for very long. My heart began to beat fast and hard.

The driver stopped abruptly near the front door.

A policeman opened the car door and got out. He walked in the direction of the front door. *He's so tall and big—bigger than my dad,* I thought. His tall, thin hat, decorated with a brass eagle, made him look taller than he actually was. He was dressed in the uniform worn by all policemen in the Third Reich.

What can I do now? I wondered.

The policeman turned around and said something to his partner. The man shook his head in agreement. I felt sick at my stomach.

With his pistol on his right hip, his billy club hanging from the other hip, and his head held high, the policeman approached our front door. I closed the curtains, hoping to shut out what was about to happen.

Three times he rang the doorbell. Each ring added to my fear. Faster and harder my heart beat. I felt weak.

Vati (Daddy) walked past my room on his way to the front door. His heavy jackboots echoed through the house as he strode down the long hall. The thump turned to a clanging sound when he marched across the marble foyer to the front door.

Berta must be gone, I thought. She always answered the door.

I got out of bed and hurried down the hall, anxious to see what would happen. Dressed in his SS uniform, my father reached for the door handle. He wore his uniform even when he was home on leave—in keeping with his very formal nature. Under the gray-green uniform jacket he wore a light brown shirt and a dark tie. Completing the uniform were the matching trousers, gathered at the top of his black jackboots. On the left lapel of his jacket was his unit insignia. Below his upper jacket pocket hung the coveted Iron Cross. He had been decorated with this distinguished medal during World War I. On his left jacket sleeve was attached the embroidered eagle with the swastika, an identification worn by all SS personnel. His shoulder and collar decorations revealed his rank as major. Around his left sleeve, about three inches from the lower edge, was a band with the words SS *Hauptamt* embroidered on it. The band identified him as an officer stationed at the main SS headquarters in Berlin. Heinrich Himmler, head of the SS, maintained his offices there.

When Vati opened the door he stood straight as if at attention. The policeman looked surprised, almost startled. He stared at my father's uniform, taking in the full story of the marking—SS *Hauptamt.* Nervously he raised his arm. "Heil Hitler," he said, quickly and respectfully.

"Heil Hitler," Vati said, returning the salute.

I couldn't see my father's face, but I knew how serious he must look. His thin hair was cut short. He parted it on the right side and kept it neatly in place with a heavy dose of hair oil. His brown eyes were always serious. Often I had the feeling that he was looking straight through me. Positioned over his right eye was the fashionable monocle. He had a broad nose, typically German. Most of the time he held his mouth closed tightly with the bottom lip protruding a little.

The policeman could not help but notice the deep scar on the left side of Vati's face. It started on the left side of his nose, slanted down to the edge of his jaw, and then came back along the jaw to stop just below the left corner of his mouth. He was proud of that scar. He had been quite a fencer during his university days. The scar was a reminder of those days, a mark of the elite men of his era. It intensified his already stern look.

The policeman looked like a man willing to forget about his errand. But with a quiver in his voice, he made the request.

"I look for Traugott Vogel to come to the Hitler Youth meeting," he said slowly, his voice breaking.

There was a moment of silence while Vati gave him a long, hard look.

The policeman waited. He looked at my father's face. He looked at the sleeve band again.

Vati stood straighter and began to wave his arms.

"You go back," he yelled and moved forward on his right foot. The policeman stepped back, obviously alarmed.

"And tell those fellows in the Hitler Youth . . ."

Vati's voice boomed through the neighborhood.

". . . that I can educate my son."

I hoped no one heard.

The policeman blushed and tried to respond. "I—I —didn't mean to offend you," he said haltingly.

Vati said nothing. He just continued to glare at the policeman and waited for him to do something.

"Yes—yes—sir," the policeman said quietly. He turned to scurry down the steps to his waiting car. He said something to his companion as he climbed in. Immediately the driver started the engine, put the car in gear, and backed out the driveway slowly.

Vati stood in the doorway to watch the car leave. He turned, and I could see his side view. His mouth was closed tightly; his expression remained harsh.

I ran to my bedroom because I knew he wouldn't appreciate my snooping. I dashed to the bedroom window and pulled back the curtains just as the police car approached the road. The two men looked very grim.

Vati sure scared them away, I chuckled to myself and got back in bed. I was scared to death of the police. I would never dare cross them. So I was sure my father must be a really powerful person if he could tell them what to do.

Vati stopped by my room on his way back to the study and came up to my bed. I opened my eyes, feigning sleepiness.

"Are you feeling better, Traugott?" he asked.

"A little," I said.

He patted me on the head. "You'll be all right tomorrow." He was more tender than he looked.

The Hitler Youth authorities never again sent the

police after me. In fact, nobody tried to tell me what to do. I enjoyed the status, but I did not take advantage of their fears. Being a loyal German youth, I, too, was caught up in Hitler's goals for Germany. I loved the Hitler Youth organization. Through this organization I was going to help Germany go forward and regain her rightful place of power in the world. "I'm going to be an SS officer just like my dad," I told my fellow Hitler Youth many times. I was determined to reach that goal.

I was little more than a child when I became a part of the Hitler Youth. At the age of ten my parents sent me to Marquartstein, a prominent boarding school in the Alps. It was at this school that I was introduced to the Hitler Youth organization.

Marquartstein, housed in an old castle, was a school that attracted nobility. Along with an application for admission, my parents were required to submit a résumé of their backgrounds. I had no difficulty being accepted because, as the son of an SS officer, I was among the elite of society. Marquartstein welcomed me with open arms. After the war, it seemed incredible and unbelievable that most Germans wanted passionately to forget about the SS. They tried to pretend that this protection squad for Hitler never existed. But in 1940, at Marquartstein, they did not feel that way.

Marquartstein was highly regimented. Run by the Third Reich, the school was clearly a training ground for those who would participate in and promote the rise of Germany. All the teachers shared a common philosophy, and they took advantage of every possible opportunity to train us in the Nazi way. Since we were living at the school, the influence of the Hitler Youth ideals and way of life was more intense than it was at public school. Life was a constant experience of indoctrination.

As a regular part of the teaching program, we often heard quotes from *Mein Kampf*. With great pride a teacher would read from the book and then add,

"This wisdom is from the great book *Mein Kampf* by Adolph Hitler." Since the book was much too deep for boys our age, we were not encouraged to read it. Our teachers interpreted the book for us.

We studied the life of Hitler in great detail. Periodically, Nazi leaders came to give speeches in which they presented their plan for Germany. They showed us what Hitler could do for us while they denounced democracy and Communism as unworkable approaches to government. And of course the Jews were a large part of our troubles. They were conspiring to take over the world, we were told. We had to stop them! "Germany's future depends on you, the youth." The leaders impressed this conviction upon us in many ways.

From time to time we marched in parades sponsored by the Hitler Youth organization. As a climax to one of these parades, I took the oath that made me an official member of the Hitler Youth. It was April 20, Hitler's birthday. In an impressive ceremony that included torchlights and candles, each new member of the Hitler Youth made a vow:

> *I promise*
> *in the Hitler Youth*
> *to do my duty*
> *at all times*
> *in love and faithfulness*
> *to the Führer*
> *so help me God.*

This oath was repeated by new members every April 20, even in 1945, less than one month before Germany surrendered to the Western Allies.

On the first of May and on January 30, we also had parades. The first of May was the national socialistic day of labor. On that day we celebrated the rule of the country by the common people—workers and farmers, not the capitalists. Often the holiday was used as an opportunity to keep us aware of the Jewish menace. Poster slogans such as "Come, dear May, and make us free from the Jews" were common sights during this observance.

January 30, 1933 marked the beginning of Germany's national revolution. As a result of a number of political victories, on that day Hitler waas appointed Chancellor of Germany. With this victory the youth of Germany came into their own. The old parties were put down, and the new Nazi Party emerged the victor. Each January 30, as we celebrated Hitler's rise to power, we, the youth of Germany, were told, "You are a powerful force in our nation's destiny."

In all these special observances, we marched to the loud, rhythmic beat of a band of drummers. In columns we marched behind the drummers who led us to a platform in the courtyard of the castle. From this elevated platform trumpeteers signaled the arrival of a party man of high rank. Standing on the wooden platform above us, the leader expounded on the glories of the Nazi Party. At these parades were such men as Baldur von Schirach, head of the Hitler Youth for all of Germany, and Heinrich Himmler, head of the SS. Always the speakers were persuasive and impressive. We all felt great pride in being part of such a grand meeting. The leaders increased our enthusiasm for the fatherland and made us want to help Hitler succeed.

Many activities of the Hitler Youth were designed to develop a team spirit. Actually, there was more emphasis on team accomplishments than individual achievement. In one war game we were divided into the Blues and the Reds. One team member was given the swastika flag. The opposing team was supposed to capture the flag and keep it for a certain length of time.

On one occasion, the teacher gave the flag to a boy nicknamed Bear, a Blues team member. We of the Reds team were in a line facing them, about fifty feet away. The teacher blew the whistle, and we all ran for Bear. Before we got to him, his teammates formed a ring to protect him. On signal we all rushed to one spot of the ring. We broke the ring and started grabbing for Bear.

"Push 'em back," someone shouted. "Get around Bear."

Two of the Reds got to Bear.

"Where is it?" one shouted.

"I don't know," the other responded. "I can't see it."

Bear's teammates managed to get around him again and push the two away. We grabbed in between the members of the protection squad, hoping to get the flag. The other teammates were pulling us away. I made one quick grab for Bear's shirt. A button flew off and a red piece of material stuck out.

It's got to be the flag, I thought. *It's got to be.* I snatched the material and ran toward the woods behind the field where we were playing. No one came after me. The two teams just kept on fighting and yelling.

I ran as fast as I could, dodging trees and going deeper and deeper into the woods. I didn't hear anyone behind me. Finally I stopped and looked around. Nobody had followed. How strange it seemed.

I listened for sounds, but there was nothing but the rustle of trees and the chirping of birds. I sat down, put my head in my hands, and rested for a minute. I had no idea of which way to start walking.

I stood up and turned around, trying to decide where I was. There were trees in all directions. *How did I get so far?* I wondered.

Suddenly a shrill sound penetrated the forest. I recognized the sound. It was a whistle, the signal that the time limit was up. The game was over. I moved in the direction of the whistle.

The loud voice of the teacher came through. I couldn't hear his words, but I knew what he would be saying. "Get in line. Stand at attention." And, as usual, he would give his command like any other grouch.

I continued to move in the direction of the sounds.

"Who has the flag?" the teacher inquired.

Everyone looked around. They could see that no one had the flag. I was close enough to hear most of what he was saying.

"Come on, boys, the teacher chided. "The game is over. Somebody must have the flag. It didn't just disappear."

"Not me," several boys responded, one after another.

"This is disgusting," he said impatiently. "Absolutely disgusting! All right, we'll stay here until somebody decides to tell where it is."

"That's not fair," a Reds team member argued. "We never got it from them."

"You must have," Bear yelled defiantly, pointing an accusing finger at the Reds team. "It's not under my shirt anymore."

"All right, boys, quit arguing," the teacher commanded.

"Sir, sir, Vogel's not here," someone shouted. "Where is he?"

No one said anything. They just looked around. By this time, I was at the edge of the forest, and I could see the crowd.

"Where is Vogel?" someone said again.

I stood behind a tree, enjoying the mystery.

"Let's go find him," one boy suggested.

I ran out of the forest, waving the flag. "Yea, yea, the winner," my teammates shouted, jumping up and down.

I was proclaimed hero of the day, but that particular strategy was a one-time occurrence. For no one became a hero in that way again. No one had used it before, and no one dared try it again.

A routine we practiced to prepare us for battle was a "take a hill" exercise. Our group leader stood at the top of a hill. When he blew the whistle, we began to climb. As we came up the hill, the leader called out the names of the ones he saw. We were supposed to get to him without being seen. Very few succeeded, but it was fun to try.

Every day was full at Marquartstein. We rose early, went to school, and did our routines and projects in the afternoon. Once in a while we had a fight. A traditional fight was over a girl who attended the girls' school nearby. At times two Hitler Youth fought for a girl of their choice. The winner won a date with the girl. Even romance was touched by the philosophy of the survival of the fittest.

In the evenings we gathered around our radios to listen to news of the glorious victories of our German soldiers. A familiar tune signaled the beginning of a special announcement. It was the song of the submarine cruise:

> *We are driving;*
> *We are driving;*
> *Against England.*

Then came the announcements:
> *February 12, 1941*
> German troops land in Tripoli, Africa.
> *August 21, 1941*
> Battle of Gomel (Russia) is finished.
> 84,000 prisoners taken. 848 guns taken.
> *August 22, 1941*
> Since the beginning of the war against the Soviet Union 1,250,000 prisoners taken; 14,000 tanks; 11,250 planes.

Later these announcements were printed in the official publication of the German Supreme Command, *The German Armed Forces Die Wehrmacht.* This publication contained reports by war correspondents, along with a picture commentary on the war. The information confirmed what our teachers told us.

Always Germany was out in front, even to the very end of the war.

"We're going to rule the world," my roommate said one evening when the announcements were over.

"We are the best!" we said in unison, smiling, confident.

"A sound body produces a sound mind" was the prominent emphasis in the Hitler Youth. All the activities pointed to that goal. In addition to our war games, we hiked a great deal and participated in all kinds of physical exercise. And we marched and marched:

.... zwei drei vier. Hup two three four.

.... zwei drei vier. Hup two three four.

The command still rings in my ears.

We had a favorite song that we sang as we marched and as we participated in parades:

Swastika on the steel helmet

Black-white-red band

Storm troopers, section Hitler

We are called.

We were going forward with Hitler, we were sure. Several years later, as I sat in a foxhole, cold, hungry, and discouraged, I wondered where we were going or where we could go.

2
Gottglaubig

Heidelberg, the "pearl" of Germany, was the place of my birth. This beautiful city, situated near the mouth of the Neckar River in southern Germany, is noted for its university and its beautiful castle which sits on the hills above the city. Since I lived in Heidelberg for only one year, my impressions of the city are limited to those of any other visitor. I have no boyhood experiences to remember about the place of my birth.

In keeping with a tradition begun in the eighteenth century, my parents named me Karl Traugott Vogel, the fifth in a line to bear the name. Unlike the American custom of adding suffixes such as Jr. to designate the bearer of the name, we in Germany passed the name on without any additions. No distinction was made between father and son. My father and I both were Karl Traugott Vogel.

Traugott, which literally means "trust God," was originally intended as a call to trust God; possibly the first person in the family line who bore the name accepted it as such a challenge. However, somewhere along the way the meaning was lost. Traugott meant nothing more than a name to me. And it meant nothing more to my parents; they gave the name to me simply to carry on a family tradition.

Practically a confirmed bachelor before he married, my father was forty-five years old when I was born. He was already firmly established as a successful industrialist. A self-made man, he had risen to the prestigious position of director of Portland Cement Company.

Educated at the Universities of Marburg, Leipzig, Göttingen, and Tübingen, my father had earned a doctor's degree in political science. In World War I he had been a first lieutenant in the Bavarian cavalry; and because of outstanding service he was decorated with the Iron Cross of the first and second class. After the war he was selected to be a representative to the Armistice talks. He told me about seeing President Wilson at those meetings.

In the 1931 edition of the Reich's *Handbook of the German Society,* my father was listed as one of the outstanding men of Germany. Hitler was listed in that same publication, along with leading Jews such as Martin Buber, the professor at Frankfurt, and Albert Einstein.

My mother, Maria Margarete Ratazzi Vogel, was born in Sydney, Australia. Her mother was German; her father was of Italian descent. By special arrangements her parents had been married in New York City, although they never lived there. My grandmother's sister who happened to live in New York helped make preparations for the wedding. Grandfather Ludwig Ratazzi was a consul to Australia, representing the tri-confederate of Germany, Austria-Hungary, and Italy.

Reared in elegant surroundings, my mother knew of no life-style other than that of the wealthy. She attended the best boarding schools in Germany, Italy, and Switzerland. At the time of her death she spoke six languages. Often during my grandfather's term as consul she stood in as hostess for my grandmother, who was in poor health.

Before meeting my father, my mother was married to a wealthy Dutch businessman named Eli van Thyn, who owned a large sugar factory in Java. In the colonial setting in which they lived she had many servants and every luxury that money could buy. My mother had been used to so much that, after the war when we were without a home of our own, wealth, or position, I was surprised that she was able to manage so well.

During the seventh year of their marriage van Thyn fell victim to a tropical disease. Several months after his death, my mother went to Holland and stayed there for a very short time. Then she moved to Wiesbaden, Germany, where her mother lived. My grandparents had bought a home in Wiesbaden in 1924 when they returned to Germany from Australia.

My parents met at a big ball in Wiesbaden and were married after a short courtship. At the wedding Vati wore his Iron Cross decoration. Soon after the wedding they bought a home in Heidelberg, where my father was director of the Portland Cement Company.

In 1931, when I was one year old, we moved to Munich, where Vati went into business with a partner. They registered a patent for a concrete railroad tie that could hold up under the movement of a train without breaking. A number of years after registering the patent, they sold it at a considerable profit.

Our home in Munich was elegant. Each of the twelve rooms was lavishly decorated in a particular period furniture. Every item in each room matched perfectly. This house was damaged in the war but has been rebuilt.

Because of their wealth and position, my parents were a part of German high society. Mutti dressed in the style and elegance of the wealthy, and Vati always looked like the typical aristocratic German. He customarily wore a gray dress suit, a white shirt with a starched collar, and a striped tie. And in keeping with German fashion, he wore the monocle over his right eye. Often, for special social occasions, Vati wore his officer's uniform from World War I. It was an honor to be able to wear the uniform, a mark of distinction. Except for his hunting outfit, I don't recall seeing my father without formal dress. He was always dressed to receive guests or to be a guest.

Naturally, my sister, Maria, and I were expected to conform to our elite status. On one occasion our nanny reprimanded me for talking to the garbage man.

"Don't ever talk to him again," she told me firmly.

"Why?" I asked. "He's a nice man."

"We just don't do that. It's not proper," she replied.

"But it doesn't make sense," I argued.

"It may not make sense to you, but don't talk to him again, even if he is nice."

"All right," I agreed. I knew her instruction was official and final.

For our parents' lavish parties, Maria and I were dressed in our finest clothes. I wore short pants made of expensive velvet. A silk shirt with ruffles completed the outfit. I looked something like a page. At the beginning of a party, our parents presented us to the guests in all our finery; then we were ushered out to resume our own play activities. It was always exciting to see the important people, if only for a few minutes.

At Munich I began public school and completed the first two grades before we moved to Augsburg in 1939. In Augsburg my father bought a construction firm and a five-story home, part of which housed offices. His business partner was named Korte. Like all the other ventures my father undertook, the construction firm of Korte and Vogel was highly successful.

Although we lived in Munich longer, I consider Augsburg my hometown. Augsburg was the last place we lived before the horrors of war caused me to become a vagabond, transported and wandering from place to place. When my family came back to Germany from Austria after the war, we came first to Augsburg.

Augsburg was about fifty miles from Dachau, the location of the infamous concentration camp. But even though we were so close to the camp, we never knew what was happening there because the camp was sealed off from the outside world. The guards did come into Augsburg, but they never talked to anyone. Periodically the guards were changed so that they would not get to know anyone in the surrounding area well enough to share information. So at this short distance, we in Augsburg knew nothing of the rapes, the tortures, the ovens where so many marched to face the fire and death. Only after the war did we discover what had happened at our doorstep.

It was at Augsburg that the process began which led to my father's association with the SS. At fifty-five, he was well past the draft age and did not have to serve in the military unless he chose to do so. But, as a loyal German, he wanted to use his talents in the service of his country.

One beautiful spring day in 1939, a group of men came to our home to see Vati. Through my bedroom window I saw them come up the driveway and get out of the car. Four men in uniform marched up to the front door.

Wow, I thought. *They look so important. I wonder why they are here.* An excited feeling raced through my body. I ran out of my room and to the end of the hall.

At the sound of the bell, Berta walked from the kitchen across the living room to the front door. Her shoes made a clanging sound on the marble foyer.

"Is the doctor in?" one of the men asked in a pleasant voice.

"Yes, he is," Berta replied. Her voice betrayed a slight nervousness. "Step inside, and I'll get him," she said, holding the door open. Evidently no one had told her that these four distinguished persons had come by appointment. They stepped inside. Berta shut the door and turned to walk toward the study.

"I'll get him," I volunteered as she came past me.

"You better tend to your own business, young man," she said firmly. I knew that meant I needed to get out of sight; so I went to my room, which was next to the study.

Berta knocked on the study door.

"Yes?" Vati responded.

"Some men from the military are here to see you."

He opened the study door. "Oh, yes," he said. "I'm expecting them. Tell them I will be there in a minute. And ask them to be seated in the living room."

Berta went to the foyer to relay the message and to direct the men to the living room. Soon I heard Vati go past my room to the stairs. A few minutes later he came back past my room with the men, talking and laughing. They went into his study and shut the door.

The men talked and talked for several hours. On my way to and from playing outside, I went near the study door and tried to hear the conversation. I could hear nothing that made sense.

In the late afternoon the meeting ended. "I'll think about it," I heard Vati tell the men as they walked down the hall. "You know, though, that I'm not young anymore; and I have a family." They did not respond to his remark.

A few days later another group of uniformed men came to see my father. I answered the door this time.

"Hello, young Traugott, is the doctor in?" the SS colonel asked. I knew the man. He was Heino Juers, a neighbor and friend of the family who had been in our home many times.

"Yes, Colonel Juers. Come in," I said. "I'll get him." The group stepped inside and shut the door. I ran to the study to get my father.

"Vati, Colonel Juers and some other men are here," I said as I knocked on the door.

He opened the door. "Fine," he said and walked toward the front door. He went to the foyer, greeted the men, and led them to his study.

I stood at the front of the hall and watched the group pass by. They all looked so serious and important in their uniforms. All were high-ranking SS officers.

The men spoke to me, calling me by name; one even patted me on the head. They went into the study, closed the door, and began a conference that continued for several hours. I listened to my radio while they talked. When I heard them come out of the study, I stood outside my door to watch them leave. They were laughing and joking. Colonel Juers shook my father's hand and said, "See you later. You've made a good decision."

For the next few days my mother and father talked privately more than usual. They made sure Maria and I did not hear. We wondered what the secrecy was all about.

"I'm going to Berlin in the morning," Vati announced one evening at supper.

"Why are you going?" I asked.

"I have some business to take care of."

"Will you be gone long?" I asked.

"No, not long," he replied.

Mutti said nothing, and her manner betrayed nothing unusual. But she was not one to express her feelings openly.

Years later my father told me about the meetings. He and our visitors had discussed the possibility of his going back into the military. Because of his success as a businessman, he was well known for his organizational ability. "We need your abilities," they had told him. He was a patriotic man; he wanted to help his country.

I was playing outside with friends when Vati returned home from Berlin. At the sound of the car motor, I stopped playing to see who was coming up the driveway. "Vati's here," I shouted as he drove on up the driveway and stopped opposite the front door. I ran to greet him.

When he opened the car door I could see that he was wearing a military uniform.

"Wow," I shouted. "You look like Colonel Juers. Where did you get that?"

"In Berlin," he replied in a matter-of-fact manner. "Is your mother here?"

"Yes. In the house."

With his hat in his hand and his head held high, he marched into the house. He looked great in his uniform, so important.

In the evening Mutti told me that Vati was a captain in the SS. He was part of Hitler's protection squad.

"Really!" I exclaimed. "That's something special, isn't it?"

"Yes," she replied in a subdued tone. "It's pretty important. But everybody who serves our country is important."

"But the SS is *really* important," I insisted.

She just smiled. I could tell she was proud but didn't want to go overboard.

I couldn't wait to tell my friends. This was the most exciting news I had heard in a long time.

Obviously my father had presented, to the proper people, his and my mother's family lines. And obviously they were declared "pure." Both of them could trace their lines back over two hundred years of the Aryan race. Hitler's protection squad was composed only of those who were considered pure.

Always a formal man, my father became even more reserved and formal when he assumed his duties as an SS officer. For a short time he worked in the SS section of Augsburg. Then, because of his organizational ability, he was transferred to the main headquarters in Berlin. He was assigned to the SS *Hauptamt*, the second-highest ranking bureau in the SS organization.

The SS *Hauptamt* was the chief recruiting agency for the military (Waffen) SS. In connection with his job, my father set up an SS division in Yugoslavia. Called the Bosniaken Division, it was composed completely of Moslems. This unit was set up to fight Tito.

After Vati joined the SS we saw very little of him.
My mother, sister, and I stayed behind in Augsburg
when he went to Berlin. But in a very short time the
SS symbol became the point of reference for our family. Even though my father came home just for short
visits periodically, our lives revolved around his association with the SS organization. Now when he
drove into our driveway, the first thing I saw was a
flag with an SS symbol on it fluttering in the wind.
Along with the flag, I saw the SS symbol on the license plate preceding the numbers. These identifi-
cations were a source of pride for me. I bragged to my
friends about my SS Vati.

The recognition the SS symbol brought to my family was thrilling. Actually, I was more greedy for the
recognition than my father was. In November, 1941,
my father and I attended a memorial service for Nazi
martyrs who had participated in the unsuccessful
march in November, 1923. They had marched to support their cause. To break up the march, the military
had shot into their ranks and killed many of the
young men. Later everyone in that march came to be
considered a part of the "blood order."

After the observance some honor guards stood at
attention. When Vati and I walked by, the guards
moved their heads in a salute to him. The gesture was
impressive. I wanted to see it again. So, with great
excitement, I suggested, "Vati, let's go back by!"

My father raised his hand. His dark brown eyes
were filled with anger. "Don't ask such a thing. It's
no joke." He struck me with a stinging slap to the side
of my face.

"The martyrs are the ones who deserve the honor,"
he said sharply. "They did their duty."

I could not reply.

"Do you understand?" he demanded, leaning down
to make me look into his angry eyes.

"Yes, I understand," I said, almost in a whisper.

Along with the other identifying marks, the Nazi Party came to have its own expression of religion. At first they were subtle in their approach. The German High Command bragged about the exactness of our bombing raids. They were so exact, they said, that an entire section of a city would be bombed, but a church would be left standing. While they boasted of such reverence for the church, all high-ranking SS officers were being asked to sever their connections with the church and join the SS religion.

In an official declaration, my father affirmed that he and all the members of his family had left the state church. At that time religious instruction was still held in the school; however, because of his declaration, I was excused from the religious instruction. I was *Gottglaubig.*

Gottglaubig, literally translated, means God believing. It was a revival of the worship of the old Germanic pagan gods, a symbol of German power. This cult emphasized the Nazi goal of reviving that German power. The Nazi swastika was a symbol that had been used by the German pagans in worship at a time when Germany was strong.

My father bought many books that dealt with the exploits of the old Germanic gods, and I was free to read them anytime I wanted to. So by the hour I read about Sigfried, who, among other things, killed a giant and a dragon who were holding a princess captive. I read about the adventures of some of the other gods, too, but Sigfried was my favorite.

We of the *Gottglaubig* had our own way of celebrating Christmas along with the traditional observance. Like most Germans, we opened our gifts on Christmas Eve or the eve before *Julfest,* as we called it in Germany. In our living room we had a very simply decorated tree. We attached candles to the ends of the branches and decorated the tree with wooden figurines of such persons as a baker, butcher, and snowman. We had no tinsel, colored ornaments, or artificial snow. In comparison to the elaborate decorations used on Christmas trees today, ours were extremely plain.

"Ding, ding, ding" signaled the time for gathering in the living room to open gifts. At the appointed time Mutti rang the bell. I banged on Maria's door as I ran to the living room. Maria caught up with me before I got there. Vati took his time. Only the four of us were there for the celebration, since the other members of our family group were not *Gottglaubig*.

We sat down beside the tree in the dimly lit room. Mutti handed Vati several matches. He lit one, stood up, and held the flame to the highest candle on the tree. The flame cast a shadow on the wall behind the tree.

"This first candle," he said, "is for all the brave men who have given their lives for our country. They were willing to die so that Germany could rise to her rightful place among the nations."

I remembered the experience at the memorial service for the Nazi martyrs who died in the 1923 march. I felt a little guilty for wanting recognition that they deserved. They had demonstrated their bravery. I had not.

Vati struck a second match and lifted it to a candle on the next branch. His words this time were for the living—those who were going forth to achieve Germany's goals. "We who survive the battle will enjoy life because of the sacrifices of others. We are marching speedily to our goal."

I felt an excitement rush through my body. It was thrilling to be a part of such a grand undertaking. I couldn't wait to be old enough to show what I could do.

Vati lit a third candle. "This candle is for the family," he said proudly. Granddaddy Vogel was the first person he named. "I knew him for only seven years," he began, "but he made a deep impression on my life. He showed me that hard work and determination can bring success. I wish all of you could have known him." He paused for a second, then added solemnly, "He was a great man."

I, too, had always wished that I had known Granddaddy Vogel.

Next Vati said a few words about Grandmother Vogel. She had reared him alone. "She inspired and encouraged me to do something worthwhile with my life," he told us. "I loved her very much."

Grandmother Vogel died when I was four years old. Each Christmas I was sorry that I had not known her longer.

Words about my mother's parents came next. Vati had never met Granddaddy Ratazzi because he had died some years before he and Mutti met. But we had pictures of him. He was a handsome man, of medium height with dark hair and eyes. His most prominent feature, as far as I was concerned, was his bushy, handlebar mustache. In most of the pictures, he looked like an aristocratic Italian in the formal dress of an official of the consulate. He was such a pleasant-looking man. I felt cheated that I had not known him.

When Vati said his few words about Grandmother Ratazzi, I pictured her Frankfurt home, which she bought in 1925 just after Granddaddy Ratazzi died. The house was exquisite. And the furnishings were even more beautiful than the structure. She had many fancy, valuable, and breakable things in her home. One room was filled with costly items imported from China. All this elegance made my visits to her home rather unpleasant. It seemed that all I ever heard was "Don't touch that. It is very fragile. Watch out; you'll knock that off. Are your shoes clean?" The nagging was constant. One time at her house I got my cousin's finger caught in a mangle. I was quickly reprimanded and told once more to leave things alone.

Along with her touchiness, Grandmother Ratazzi never trusted anyone. The only rooms she left open were four big rooms that were used for entertaining and eating. She always carried a ring of keys that fit the doors to all the rooms she kept locked.

From grandparents, my father proceeded to say words about my mother's family. Since he was an only child, Vati had no other person in his family to mention. He remembered my mother's younger brother, Carlo. Carlo had been born an Australian. But during the war he worked for the Germans. In so doing, he had committed treason. His wife was the daughter of a white Russian officer. Two months after the war ended, the two of them were found dead in their home in Berlin.

My father's words for Carlo and his wife, Lucia, were complimentary. He was glad this brother chose to align himself with the Germans.

During the war Mutti's other brother, Leo, was a major in the British royal medical corps. His home was heavily damaged by German bombers. My father never talked about Uncle Leo.

The division in loyalties was always a source of deep agony for my mother. She was a woman torn between two countries, two allegiances. On the one hand, her husband and brother were entirely dedicated to a cause. On the other hand, another brother whom she also loved was equally convinced that his side was right.

Rarely did my mother express her feelings about the divided family. Only during the times of deep sorrow and distress did she break down and talk about what the war did to her and her family. And even then the outburst was brief, possibly only a sentence. Toward the end of the war the strain was evident in her face. She lived for twenty-eight years after the war ended, but she died a woman who had not found real peace.

As the candles flickered and cast shadows on the wall, Vati said a few words about the four of us. "I am glad we can be together, if for just a short time," he began. "I hope our future will be filled with ac-

complishments for our family and for our homeland."
He expressed special pride in the fact that we were
winning the war and that we were in control of most
of Europe. Through his eyes the future looked bright
indeed—in 1940.

After the candlelighting observance, we opened our
gifts that Mutti had arranged attractively on our long
table. Each of us had a section of the table designated
for our gifts. When Vati concluded his remarks about
the family, he and Mutti removed the tablecloth that
had covered the gifts for several days. As we opened
the gifts, we expressed thanks and surprise. How happy Christmas always was. "This is just what I
wanted," we all said over and over.

Although my mother had been reared a Catholic
and my father was a Lutheran until he joined the SS,
there was no religious observance connected with
our Christmas celebration. We did not read the Bible.
The one Bible we owned, which my parents had received when they married, was stuffed away in a
drawer or in some remote corner of the bookcases. I
didn't know for sure. We did not mention Christ.
We did not voice a prayer. We had our own SS expression of religion. We were *Gottglaubig*.

3
Setting Things Straight

We are driving;
We are driving;
Against England.

The familiar tune arrested my attention. A special announcement was coming. In the winter of 1943-44 the reports of outstanding victories for our side were still coming across the waves. I was fourteen then. The accounts of the many prisoners taken, as well as guns, tanks, and planes, were a source of special pride. Who in the world was as strong as Germany? No one doubted that we were winning the war—at least no one I knew. It was only a matter of time, we assumed, before our leaders would sound the news of a complete victory. Still, deep down, we did have some questions, some fears.

So far Augsburg had not been touched by the destruction. We lived with the fear, though, that it could be bombed at any time because we knew that a number of German cities had been hit. That was just a part of war. So why should we escape?

The date was February 24, 1944. I was in my room talking with friends when the air-raid warning sounded that cold winter morning.

"What was that?" Manfred exclaimed.

"Just what you think," I replied, "the air-raid warning. You guys better get home."

The three boys ran out of the room, down the hall, and out the front door. I followed them to the door and stepped outside to take a quick glance at the sky. The boys ran on to their homes a short distance away.

Where are the planes? I wondered. There were none in sight. "They must be far away," I said out loud.

Mutti came through the door that I had left open. "Come on in, Traugott," she said impatiently. "Hurry, hurry! The planes will be here any minute."

"But where are they?" I asked as I came in the door.

"Just outside town, probably," she replied. "Come on, let's get to the cellar. Here, put your coat on; it will be cold down there." She threw the coat around my shoulders.

We hurried down the narrow stairs to find that Maria and Berta were already there, huddled in the darkest corner of the damp room. We sat down beside them.

"Where are they?" I asked again.

"They'll be here soon," Mutti answered, adding as an afterthought, "unless it's a false alarm."

"I hope it is," Maria said nervously.

"I was sure we would win the war before it came to Augsburg," Berta said, shaking her head.

"I thought the planes just came at night," I questioned. "Why are they coming during the day when our gunners can see them?"

"What gunners?" Mutti commented. "What made . . ."

She didn't finish. Suddenly we heard the overpowering roar of the bombers.

"Here they come," Maria cried, burying her head in her hands. "Ooooh . . . No!"

"Don't worry," Mutti said, putting her arm around Maria's shoulder. "We'll be all right. We're well protected."

We all sat there paralyzed, waiting for the bombs to fall, trying to believe that we were well protected.

But nothing happened. The bombers went on over,

and soon we could hear the roaring sound no more. They were gone.

"Maybe they're our own planes," Berta suggested.

"That would be a crazy mistake," Mutti said, "sending us to the cellar when our own planes come."

"Guess so," Berta replied. "But why didn't they do anything?"

"Maybe it's not over yet," Maria moaned.

"I . . ."

The clearance signal interrupted Berta's remark. Immediately we jumped up and went outside to see what had happened. We joined the crowd that was forming in the street. All of us looked around for signs of bombers, but there was no evidence in our neighborhood. The houses were not damaged. There was no fire.

"Look," someone said. The man pointed south. "The Messerschmidt Works."

We all looked in that direction. The Messerschmidt Aircraft Works, home of the most famous German fighter, the M.E. *109,* was engulfed in flames. Smoke billowed to the sky.

Within a few seconds the deafening sounds of sirens came from all directions. Almost by instinct, I ran toward the fire station in our area. I met other boys along the way. We of the Hitler Youth were assigned firefighting duty. As we rounded the corner the fire truck was pulling out of the station.

"Wait! Wait!" we yelled and waved our arms.

"Wait! Wait!"

The men on the truck signaled to the driver, and he stopped to let us on. Then through the streets of Augsburg we raced, with sirens going full blast. The truck went so fast that the people along the route were one big blur. And the speed made the winter breeze more bitter than ever. I pulled my coat tight around me to ward off the cold, but there was little relief. By the time we got to the Works my nose was frozen, and my eyes were watering.

We jumped down from the trucks and helped the

firemen with the hoses. "It's almost gone," one man remarked. "They really hit it."

Everywhere we looked there was fire, jumping in large billows to the sky, one after another. The heat from the flames brought some relief from the cold.

The fire was almost out of control when we got there, and the bitter cold added to the almost impossible task. Water froze as it came out of the hoses. We worked hard, but the plant was completely destroyed.

"No planes will be built here anytime soon," a firefighter muttered.

"I'm afraid you're right," another agreed. "This is a mess."

It was several hours before the fire was under control; and even then little fires kept erupting. Shortly after noon they dismissed us of the Hitler Youth because they felt that the regular crew could take care of things.

Walking home, we speculated on what would happen next. Was this all the enemy wanted in Augsburg, or was there more to come?

"If they can get through during the day," someone suggested, "they sure can get through at night."

"Yeah," we all agreed.

"Where is our protection?" one asked.

That night we received the answer to that question.

Just after dark we heard the whirring sound of the air-raid warning. For the second time in one day we made our way down the narrow stairway leading to the cellar. The sounds of running on the stone steps echoed through the house as the air-raid warning penetrated the walls. Again we huddled in one corner of the cellar to wait for other sounds.

"I knew they'd be back," Berta said with resignation. "But I hoped they wouldn't."

"Me too," Mutti added. "War is terrible ... terrible."

"I hear them; I hear them," Maria cried. "It can't be; it can't be. Two times in one day. It's too much."

It came nearer and nearer—the terrifically loud, grinding roar of the bombers. The sounds of the air-raid warning were silenced.

"There are a lot more this time!" I exclaimed. "And they're everywhere."

I was sitting between Mutti and Maria. They both trembled. My heart beat hard and fast. The bombers came closer and closer.

"They're not going to leave this time," Berta murmured. "This is the real thing. I just can't believe it."

"I'm afraid," Maria shivered. She began to cry.

Bombs began to fall. Mutti put her head in her hands. I, too, couldn't believe it was all happening. I had heard about the blockbusters—bombs that could level an entire block. Now I heard them fall. I was overcome with terror, but I had to be brave.

We heard the shriek of a bomber flying near. Then the house shook as a horrendous roar tore through the walls. Our home had been hit!

"Oh, no!" Mutti shrieked. She began to cry.

"No, no!" Berta screamed and ran to the stairs that led outside. I ran after her and grabbed her arm just as she reached the door.

"Where are you going?" I yelled.

"Outside! Outside! Let me go!"

"You can't go, Berta," I said, trying to be calm. "You've got to stay here."

"But we'll all be killed. We'll burn. Let me go! Let me go!"

I hung onto her arm tightly and pleaded with her. "Berta, this is the safest place. You'll be killed for sure outside."

"I'd rather be killed out there than in here," she sobbed.

"But you have a chance in here. They'll be gone before the fire gets down here. Then we can get out. Just calm down." I really didn't believe what I was saying.

I pulled at her arm and led her down the stairs to

the corner where Mutti and Maria were still huddled. Paralyzed with fear, we all sat close together, trembling, crying, wondering if we could survive.

The bombing was endless. "Will it ever stop," I sighed.

"Hey, I think they're leaving," Mutti exclaimed.

The bombs had quit falling, and the sound of the bombers grew faint. The enemy had gone. In a few minutes, when the clearance signal sounded, we climbed out of the cellar. Then for a time we stood back from the house surveying the scene. Fire shot out of most of the windows. The top floors, which housed offices and apartments, were going fast.

"We must save what we can," Mutti said with agony in her voice. "We can't let everything go up in flames."

Some people came to help. Two men carried a bed; another carried a chair. Another brought out a table. There was no plan. Each person just took what he could. It was utter panic.

I ran in the front door and down the hall to my father's study. The curtains were burning. Quickly I pulled them down and snuffed out the fire. This room meant so much to me. Often I had gone in there alone when Vati was away. The books and surroundings fascinated me. Sometimes I read the papers on the desk, but they seldom made sense. I took out books that interested me. The books were all uniformly bound with various colors of leather designating the subject matter. Blue was for history, green for hunting, brown for literature, and red for philosophy. Usually I gravitated toward history. I studied the pictures of the soldiers and looked forward to the day when I could be a part of that exciting life. I always felt that my father was doing something great, and I wanted to join him in that mission.

I started grabbing—books, oil paintings, picture albums. When my arms were full I ran down the hall, out the door, and threw the items on the lawn. The

Bible my parents received when they married was mixed in with the other books that lay there. *Mein Kampf* went up in the flame.

I ran back to the study. The contrast between the bitter cold outside and the heat inside made the heat even more intense. On the second trip I took out some chairs. I wanted to drag the inlaid desk out, but it was too heavy. A third trip to the study was out of the question. The desk went up in flames.

On the second trip out, as I passed the living room, I saw the large painting of my father which was practically life size. He was dressed in his fancy hunting outfit. On his head he wore a top hat with a wide ribbon band decorating it. His shirt was light brown and his tie multicolored. His vest and pants were a dark brown; the jacket was a shade lighter. On his belt he had an oversized brass buckle, elaborately engraved. Hanging with a strap across his left arm was his hunting gun. He held his left hand in position just above his waist to display the family seal ring, which was on his ring finger.

I put the chairs down outside and ran back to the living room. Carefully I removed the picture from the wall—the last item that I saved from the flames. The intense heat of the fire drove me back when I tried to go in again. Today that picture decorates a wall in my dining room.

The firefighters came; but when they sprayed water on the outside walls the remaining structure froze, just as it had at the Messerschmidt Works. They kept trying, though. As they worked I looked up and down the street. As far as I could see, houses were burning. The heat was so intense that the asphalt pavement melted and ran everywhere. In the distance the onion dome of a church building fell to the ground like a giant fireball. The sight was overwhelming.

I looked at our house again and again. Everything that seemed so precious was being destroyed. I fought back the tears. Most of the elegant, beautiful, costly furniture was gone, I was sure. We saved my parents' ivory-colored bed with the gold trim, but the matching pieces were gone. In comparison to what we had owned, the items gathered on the front lawn were so few—so very few.

Finally our house quit burning. How, I'm not sure, because very little water actually got to the flames. The outer frame stood; but inside, the house was practically hollow down to the first floor. We spent the night in the cold, damp cellar, sleeping on the beds and covers that we had managed to save.

"The war has come to our doorstep," Mutti said as we made our beds.

"What will we do now?" Maria asked.

"We'll just have to wait and see what the state says. We can't live here."

"We sure can't," I responded. "This is terrible."

"But for now," Mutti suggested, "let's go to bed."

For the first time we realized that the total war was upon us; and it was not a good feeling. To add to our depression, we discovered that our school was completely destroyed. But in a way it didn't matter; so many houses were destroyed that there would have been no kids around to go to the school, anyway.

The destruction was hard to believe. House after house—entire blocks—were in ruins. Many homes were burned to the foundation with nothing saved. For a few days families crowded together in the structures that still stood. We stayed in our cellar, along with the family who lived next door.

Within two days after the bombing Vati was in Augsburg, and we all went inside the ruins together. Impulsively I started up the stone steps inside.

"Get down from there," Vati called after me. "You have nothing to hang on to." The wooden rail had burned away.

"It will take a lot to rebuild this, but it can be done," Vati remarked when we went back outside.

"The outside structure is good." Then he turned to me. "Traugott, you stay outside because the house is dangerous. The floors are weak and things could fall at any time."

"Are you hearing that?" Mutti added.

"Yes, I am."

"What a shame," Vati sighed, almost to himself. Then turning around to us, he said in a tone of resignation, "But this is the price we have to pay. Many have suffered in the same way. Every German should be willing to sacrifice. It's the only way we can win." Apparently he had no second thoughts.

That evening I sat on the back steps and thought . . . and thought. "Ooooh, I hate them! I hate them!" I whispered over and over. The tears rolled down my cheeks. As darkness fell, the ruins looked even more ominous. I hated everyone who had caused this terrible thing to happen—the Americans, British, French, Russians, and . . . the Jews. I had nothing because of them.

Within a week we were evacuated to a village outside town. The few possessions we had saved were boxed and sent to friends and to our hunting lodge in Austria. Vati stayed in Augsburg until the relocation was complete.

For a brief period of time there were no regular school hours. I missed school. I missed our house and the surroundings. I missed Berta, who had gone to work in a factory.

Every chance I got, I went into Augsburg to see our house. On the way I tried to pretend that the bombing never happened. Always the ruins brought me back to reality. The stately domes that had decorated the top of our house were completely gone. The outside structure of the fifth floor was missing in places. Most of the windows were broken. The balconies were ready to fall if subjected to any weight. Each visit, I walked around the grounds recalling better days. Each visit, I wished it had never happened.

Each visit, I choked back the tears. Each visit, I vowed to pay back the ones who had caused the destruction.

As soon as arrangements could be made, our entire school was evacuated to Oberstaufen, a resort area in the Alps. The boys' school was set up in a large restaurant. We were housed in two boarding houses which had been confiscated by the government, along with the restaurant. The owners retained the title to the property, but they had no say about how the facilities were used. It was wartime; everybody had to sacrifice.

Maria's school was set up in a town a long distance away from mine, so we did not see each other. Mutti went to our hunting lodge in Austria, and Vati returned to his work in Berlin and Yugoslavia. From that time, we had little choice about where we would live.

For the first time in my life, I knew what it was to want and not have. Food was not as plentiful at the school as it had been at home. Even with the war all around us, we had managed to secure the food we needed, so I was not aware of any food shortage. But at our evacuated school we got up early, cleaned our shoes, and went to a lean breakfast. Along with a glass of weak cocoa or milk, two slices of bread was the maximum offering. I was hungry most of the time.

A few of us boys were convinced that the food shortage was a farce, and we wanted to do something to solve the problem. We were sure our leaders were holding back food that we should have. After a period of grumbling, I called a meeting in my room.

"We know they're holding stuff back," I told them.

"Yeah," Fritz added. "They have no right to starve us."

"What can we do?" Erwin asked.

"I have an idea," I said. "Why don't we get some of the food and store it in our rooms? Then we could eat whenever we're hungry."

"Raid the pantry!" Ernst exclaimed. "Do you think we can get away with it?"

"Sure," Fritz assured him. "If we're quiet. Old man Schmidt won't wake up."

"What about Mrs. Schmidt?" Erwin asked.

"That's the reason we need to be quiet. She sleeps with one eye open."

"How do you know?" I asked.

"Somebody told me," Fritz replied. "But we can go barefooted and make it all right."

"What if they catch us?" Erwin asked. "What will they do to us?"

"Don't worry, Erwin, they won't catch us," Fritz said confidently.

"Besides, my father's an SS officer. They'll be afraid to do anything to me and my friends," I added.

"Yeah," Fritz agreed.

"So are we all agreed we're going to do it?" I asked.

"Yeah," Erwin said confidently.

"Sure," Fritz and Ernst chimed in.

"Let's go ahead and do it tonight then. After ten o'clock bed check. We'll wait until everyone is asleep. Then I'll knock twice on your wall, Fritz. All right?"

"All right. Ernst and I will meet you and Erwin in the hall."

After the meager evening meal, we were more determined than ever to go through with our plan. The four of us shared knowing glances all during the meal.

As usual, Mr. Schmidt came around for the ten o'clock bed check. When the time seemed right, I tapped on the wall. The four of us met in the hall and sneaked down the stairs, through the kitchen, and into the pantry. No one uttered a word, not even a whisper. Inside the pantry, we were overwhelmed with the sight.

"Would you look at that!" Fritz exclaimed in a whisper.

The shelves were full—canned fruit, all kinds of jams, crackers—everything.

"All this, and we are starving," Ernst said with disgust.

"Don't talk out loud," I cautioned. "They'll know we're here."

"Where do we start?" Erwin asked.

"Let's take the big pails of jam first," I suggested.

Each of us lifted a pail of jam off the shelves, walked through the kitchen, and headed for the stairs. We looked around as we started climbing the stairs. There were no signs of anyone stirring.

We hid the jam in our closets and met in the hall once more. "Let's get some crackers and fruit this time," I said as we started for the stairs. "Where's Fritz?"

"He's already down there," Ernst said. "I told him to wait, but he was anxious to get some more."

Halfway down the stairs, we heard a scream. "Hey!" It was Mrs. Schmidt's voice.

"She's got Fritz," I gasped.

"Let's get out of here before she sees us," Ernst whispered.

"Fast," I added.

We ran to our rooms and jumped in bed. I was trembling all over. I couldn't be sure we got away before she saw us.

In a few minutes we heard a knock. "Is that our door?" Erwin gasped.

"No. It's across the hall. Be quiet."

"Come downstairs right now," someone ordered. It was Mr. Schmidt. "Come barefooted." He went on to the next door, and the next, saying the same thing. Finally he came back up the hall to our door and gave the same command.

"Remember," I said, "we don't know anything."

Downstairs, Mr. Schmidt directed us to the porch. Like us, most of the boys were clad in shorts and an undershirt—and no shoes.

"I didn't know we would have to go out there," Erwin gasped. "It's freezing cold, and that floor is even colder."

"Boy, they're savages," I snarled.

On the porch, we joined the line that had already formed. Mr. Schmidt, standing in front of the line with his pointing stick, ordered us to stand at attention. Fritz stood by his side.

"We know," he began in his squeaky voice, "that Fritz wasn't alone. So why don't you who were his companions save us a lot of time and confess? It's late, and we all want to get back to bed."

I looked at the clock above the mantle. It was 11:30 P.M. My feet were freezing.

"We'll find out who you are when we search for the food you took."

No one spoke. The three of us looked out the sides of our eyes to see if anyone suspected. Fritz stared straight ahead.

"Are you going to let Fritz take all the blame?" Mr. Schmidt asked with disgust evident in his voice. Fritz looked so forlorn, like an abandoned child.

Mr. Schmidt held the pointing stick straight out from his waist. His eyes caught mine. The stick came hard on my shoulder and sent a sharp pain down my right arm. My mouth flew open, but I suppressed a reaction.

"Traugott," he said sharply. "What do you know about this?"

"Nothing," I replied quickly. "Nothing, sir."

He went on down the line, staring into everyone's eyes. Even the innocent felt guilty. He stopped again at the end of the line and brought the stick down hard on Albert's shoulder. He almost cried.

"Albert," Mr. Schmidt demanded. "Do you know who did this?"

"No, sir," he said, his voice cracking. "Honest!"

Mr. Schmidt started back up the line, leaning down to stare into every boy's eyes. "What do you know?" he asked over and over.

"Nothing, sir . . . nothing, sir," came the reply over and over.

My feet began to ache from the cold. We all began

to stand on one foot and then the other to ease the pain.

"Stand still," Mr. Schmidt ordered.

We stood there, our teeth chattering and our legs aching. The young ones started crying. I felt ashamed.

"All right, we'll get the paddle and start at one end of the line. Three licks for everyone until someone confesses."

Almost in unison everyone gasped. That paddle was murder. I couldn't let it happen. I stepped forward.

"I was with him," I said quietly. Erwin and Ernst followed my lead.

Mr. Schmidt shook his head in desperation. "You four stay here," he ordered. "The rest of you go back to bed and get some sleep."

He took us inside and told us to sit down on the sofa. He and his wife sat in front of us in two easy chairs. I wanted to sit on my frozen feet to warm them up, but I didn't dare.

"You know this is stealing, don't you?" Mr. Schmidt began.

"Just common thieves," his wife chimed in, shaking an accusing finger at us.

"Children should be fed right," I said defiantly. "You're holding back food from us." I rubbed my aching feet.

"It's ours," Ernst insisted.

"You must understand," Mr. Schmidt explained. "We are engaged in a war. Food is scarce. If we use up everything we have, we may not get anymore."

"So we have to ration it," Mrs. Schmidt said sharply. "It is better to have a little at a time than none at all, don't you think?" She glared at us and opened her eyes wide.

They tried to make us understand the situation, but we could not be convinced. There was food in the pantry, and we wanted to eat it.

"I'm going to write a letter to my daddy," I threatened. "He's in Berlin headquarters."

They didn't respond to my threat verbally, and they showed little emotion in their faces. But they ended the conversation soon after my remark.

"We must go to bed now," Mr. Schmidt said. "We have to get up early. Go to your rooms."

Two days later, without any explanation, I was sent to Steibis, a school located a few miles higher in the Alps. A group of teachers met and made the decision. Apparently they weren't afraid of my father.

At Steibis I set out to correct another unpleasant situation—the early-morning hours. We boys didn't like to get up at 5:30 A.M., so four of us planned to do something about it after bed check. At ten o'clock one night, as we expected, the house father came by.

"You boys in bed?" he asked as he stuck his head in the door.

"Yes, sir," we replied as we did every night.

He closed the door and went to the next room.

"I told Paul and Gustav that we would meet them in half an hour at the bottom of the stairs," I whispered.

The minutes dragged by. Except for a familiar creak here and there, soon all was quiet.

"Is it time yet?" Arthur asked impatiently.

I shone my flashlight at my watch—the watch I had received on my last birthday before the bombing. "No, not yet. Ten more minutes."

It was a long ten minutes. We stared into the darkness.

"All right, let's go," I said. "It's time."

"Great!" Arthur exclaimed in a whisper.

Carefully I opened the door, stuck my head out, and glanced up and down the hall. "It's clear; let's go."

With our shoes in our hands, we crept down the stairs. Paul and Gustav were already at the bottom, waiting quietly.

A door creaked open. "What was that?" Paul whispered.

We crouched beside the stairs. The door closed.

"Probably someone going to the bathroom," I said in a low whisper. "Come on, let's run for the door."

"Make sure the door is unlocked," Paul cautioned. "We have to get back in."

"All right," Gustav volunteered.

Safely outside, we ran to a clump of bushes down the hill to put on our shoes. As we got up to leave, we looked back at the big house. The windows reflected the light from the moon, giving the house an eerie look. The big fir tree in the front yard cast a shadow on one side of the house.

We walked in the direction of the village church. "Do you think anyone will be around the church?" Paul asked.

"At this time?" I laughed. "Certainly not. You know the people in this town. They go to bed with the chickens."

"I can't wait to see the surprised looks on the faces of our teachers," Arthur chuckled, "especially Mr. Hauser."

"What if the door is locked?" Paul suggested.

"You worry too much, Paul," Gustav advised. "It's always open. Why lock it? Who's low-down enough to steal from a church?"

The door was open, and we stepped inside.

"Who's going to go to the top?" Paul asked.

"I'm willing," Gustav volunteered.

"Me, too," I said. "You and Arthur stand guard."

"All right," Paul agreed. "We will. But hurry."

"Don't rush us," Gustav said. "It will take time."

We trudged up the narrow stairway to the top of the steeple. When we reached the top, I climbed out onto the ledge in front of the clock and began to turn the handles.

"Put it back two hours," Gustav urged.

"No, we said one hour. Remember? We couldn't get away with two hours. Someone would wake up for sure."

It was eleven-twenty. I set the clock back to ten-twenty and climbed off the ledge. Mission accomplished, we went down the stairs to join our companions.

"Anyone come by?" I asked Paul.

"No people, just a cat or two."

"Grrrrrr . . . Grrrrrr."

We reeled in the direction of the sound.

"Where did he come from?" Arthur questioned.

The big shepherd dog barked fiercely. "Stay still," I said. "If we run, he'll eat us up."

"But we can't stay here," Arthur warned. "They'll find out what we did."

"Yeah, we've got to get out of here," Paul added.

A light went on in a house across the street. "Oh, they're going to get us," Gustav gasped.

Suddenly we heard a hissing sound. Behind us was a cat. "Let him have the cat," Gustav suggested. "Let's go."

The dog went after the cat, and we headed for the school. "Boy, will it be nice to sleep until six-thirty tomorrow morning," Paul sighed.

It was about twelve-thirty when we slipped back into the house. I had no trouble going to sleep. The escapade had left me very tired.

At breakfast Mr. Hauser marched into the dining hall. Gustav leaned over to me. "Boy, look at him," he whispered. "We're in trouble."

"Not if we keep our mouths shut," I said. "How would they ever find out?"

With a stern look on his face, Mr. Hauser called us to attention. "Immediately after breakfast," he said, "we will gather in the courtyard. We have a matter to resolve."

"Wonder what it is?" the boy next to me asked. "He sure looks mad."

"Knowing him, it could be anything," I replied.

We gathered in the courtyard and stood at attention.

"As you surely have noticed," Mr. Hauser began, "we all got up an hour late this morning."

Several of the boys looked at each other in surprise. They hadn't noticed.

He continued his speech. "Some of the teachers have been ready to start classes for over an hour. They have been greatly inconvenienced," he added pompously.

Mr. Hauser frowned and looked up and down the line. He stopped at one end and gazed at the boys there.

"Rolf," he said, "did you notice anything unusual last night after you went to bed?"

"No, sir," Rolf replied with a quiver in his voice.

"Did you hear anything?"

"No, I went right to sleep."

Mr. Hauser walked to the middle of the line. "We know that several of you boys are responsible. Someone in the village saw you." My heart skipped a beat. "Albert, did you see anyone leave the house?"

"No . . . no, sir. I went right to sleep. I heard nothing."

"Gustav," he said as he moved on down the line, "what about you? Did you hear anything unusual?"

Gustav hesitated. "No . . . ."

"You went right to sleep, too, I am sure," Mr. Hauser interrupted.

Gustav looked relieved. He shook his head in agreement.

"But why are you shaking, Gustav?"

"I didn't realize I was. It is a little chilly, though." I suppressed the laughter.

Mr. Hauser took a deep breath. His eyes filled with disgust. He held his mouth tight as if gritting his teeth and shook his head back and forth. Then he began his appeal.

"Do you who did this deed want to see everyone suffer for the actions of a few?"

He kept staring at us, moving his eyes up and down the line. "We will stay here until someone confesses," he threatened.

"Oh, boy," someone said under his breath.

Mr. Hauser turned in his direction and kept staring at him. The boy looked straight ahead.

Gustav turned to me. "Let's get it over with."

"Shut up," I whispered.

"Come on, Traugott, it's not worth it."

"No! No!"

"Oh, we have a conversation going on here," Mr. Hauser said sarcastically. "Is it interesting?"

We both turned red. "Do you have something to tell me, boys?"

"I do," Gustav volunteered.

"Me, too," I said, knowing there was no way out.

Arthur and Paul stepped forward together.

Everyone stared at us. Some were holding back laughter, but I really didn't care.

"Paul, Gustav, Traugott, and Arthur, stay," Mr. Hauser ordered. "The rest of you go to your classes." He turned to me.

"Traugott, go tell Mr. Haupt that I want to see him and come back immediately."

I ran into the house to give Mr. Haupt the message and then hurried back outside. In a few minutes Mr. Haupt appeared.

"Mr. Haupt," Mr. Hauser said while we stood at attention, "you will exercise these four boys all day. They are to do whatever you say."

"Yeeees, sir. It will be a pleasure." He was bloodthirsty.

Mr. Haupt took us to a field beside the school. And at his command, we marched and marched and marched. We did the commando crawl over and over. We did knee bends fifty at a time. At lunchtime we stopped for a short time and then went back to the field to continue the exercises. Mr. Haupt didn't let up for a minute. He thoroughly enjoyed the assignment.

At the end of the day we fell into bed, exhausted. Again, going to sleep was no problem. And we had no desire to climb to any church steeple again—ever!

4
Let's Go

Aside from pranks, a typical day at the Steibis school began with classroom instruction shortly after breakfast. The process of indoctrination and instilling patriotism was woven into the total program. The atmosphere was more regimented than ever. None of us ever saw our parents, but I don't remember being homesick.

In the afternoon we undertook various projects, along with our paramilitary training. One project was a swimming pool. We dug out a large area for the pool beside the large house that was used for a dormitory. We hammered poles along the walls. To further reinforce the walls we wound branches in and out of the poles. This was a gigantic undertaking, but using the pool was a source of pride because we had constructed it ourselves.

Every night we gathered around radios to hear the reports about the war—just as we had done in the school at Oberstaufen. All the reports continued to be good news. We were still taking many prisoners, tanks, and ammunition. We were winning the war, they announced. I continued to believe them.

One morning at breakfast Mr. Hauser told us that there would be shooting matches in the afternoon. I was excited. Two years before, some of the hunters who shot game on the land surrounding our lodge had taught me how to shoot. When my father discovered that they were teaching me, he said, "Forget about it. You're too young to shoot now. You have plenty of time to learn how to be a soldier." I didn't believe him and still practiced shooting whenever I got the chance.

After the shooting match the recruiter gathered together those of us who had done well. "How would you like to go into the army?" he asked.

"Sure, sure," we all replied. "We want to."

They sent us to a camp for a three-week training course. When we first got to the camp, they issued us uniforms. What excitement! It made me feel like a real soldier. I was determined to do my best. And I earned a medal for marksmanship.

Those of us who earned the marksmanship medal were told that we would be going into the army. In December of 1944, our leaders realized that everybody was needed for the war effort. We were inducted into the *Volkssturm,* the people's army, the home guard. This was Germany's last resource—old men and boys. I was fifteen, but some were younger. Many years later I saw the grave of a twelve-year-old boy who had died in battle.

My unit was sent to what became known as the Battle of the Bulge on the western border of Germany. This was our final effort to get the Allied forces off of German territory.

Gustav and I were two of three soldiers assigned to one of the machine-gun details. We were given the task of carrying the ammunition.

From the training camp we marched north. All along the way to our post, we saw shocking evidence of the devastating effects of war. Everywhere we went the enemy had preceded us.

"Boy, there must have been a fierce battle here," a fellow soldier remarked as we entered Duren, a town along the way to our assignment. We walked down the main street of the town, dodging the shot-up jeeps and tanks. We gazed at the damaged buildings. I shivered at the sight of the many dead bodies, partially covered by snow. They were everywhere.

"We've got to get those murderers!" I exclaimed.

"Yeah," the soldier walking beside me agreed.

That first night on the road we slept in foxholes inside a forest. The forest was a few degrees warmer than the open countryside. I was glad for a little relief from the bitter cold.

All during the night we heard machine-gun fire in the distance. The sounds brought back memories of another cold winter night. Less than a year had passed since that terrifying and depressing experience in Augsburg. I relived the experience. I saw the onion dome of the beautiful cathedral fall to the ground like a giant fireball. I saw the streets aflame. I saw myself in my father's study, desperately trying to save the precious possessions. I pictured the big house in utter ruin. I choked back the tears. When would it end?

One day after traveling twenty-five miles on foot, my group came to an old house. Our leader went to the door and knocked, but no one answered. He tried the door handle and walked on in and looked around.

"Come on in," he said, waving his arms. "No one is here." It was evident that the occupants had been gone for some time.

We gathered wood from the barn, made a fire in the big fireplace, and ate the small amount of food that was left in the house. I was thankful for a place to stay that sheltered me from the bitter cold.

We kept moving toward our post. Sometimes we stayed in an area protected by barbed wire and mines. We stayed as long as three or four days in the cold foxholes waiting for the Allied forces to come. But they never came. We went out to them, but they did not come where we were.

Finally we arrived at our post, a few miles north of Monschau. The experiences there were about the same as they had been along the way. We went out to the enemy, but they did not come to us.

One day the inevitable happened—one of the guys in our group was killed. He was part of a patrol. Two of his buddies brought him in. Gustav and I were assigned the burial duty. We went down a hill behind our camp and dug a hole. When that task was finished, we wrapped the soldier in canvas and placed him in the shallow grave.

"I've never seen anyone I knew die before," I told Gustav. "I knew Erich."

"Me too," Gustav said. "Let's go," he added abruptly. He didn't want to talk about it.

We picked up our shovels and walked back up the hill in silence.

Will I be next? I thought as I huddled in the foxhole that night. *Will those dirty Americans kill me, too?* I was cold, scared, and hungry. The supply truck had not come with food during the day. I wept quietly . . . and thought.

Many times at night I had wept from exhaustion and fear. The experience of seeing Erich made the feelings more intense than they had been before. I had seen dead bodies all along the way to our post—but I didn't know who they were. They were just nameless faces. I knew Erich, and that made the difference.

The end has to be near, I thought.

Our leaders didn't acknowledge the fact. We didn't talk about the subject in large groups. But the truth was evident for those who wanted to know: We were a defeated army. It was only a matter of time.

Day after day Gustav and I followed the machine gunner from position to position, lugging the ammunition. Periodically our unit leader directed the machine gunner to point the weapon in a certain direction. Then, on command, he fired the gun. Once in a while someone fell. We didn't stop at the bodies. We just kept on moving. Except for the uniform, they looked a lot like us.

Our unit was supposed to keep the enemy from going beyond a certain line north of Monschau. Early one Friday morning a commando got through the line to bring a message. He told our leaders that an enemy unit was preparing to attack, and it was really supposed to be a tough unit. The news spread rapidly through the camp, producing its disabling effect on a group of soldiers who were ill-fed, homesick, and exhausted.

Gustav, Albert, and I found a private place to talk. We assessed the situation.

"I'll bet it's that black unit we've heard so much about," Gustav said.

"I've heard they are savages," I remarked.

For me, the black man was an unknown quantity because I had never come in contact with a black man in my life. And at a time when an enemy attack was imminent, anything unknown added to my fear.

"If we live through the attack," Gustav added, "there is no telling what they will do to us. I've heard they are vicious like you say, Traugott."

"How can we hold out at all?" Albert questioned. "We are all so exhausted; our supplies are low . . . ."

"And everyone is so discouraged," I chimed in.

We were overcome with a spirit of defeatism. So many of us were too young to be in battle.

Immediately we began preparing for the attack, setting up our positions on a hill overlooking the area we were supposed to defend. Utterly devoid of enthusiasm, we simply did what we were told to do.

The supply trucks did not come in the afternoon as we had hoped. Consequently, our evening meal was very meager again. Soon after eating we took our positions in the foxholes. The three of us assigned to the machine-gun detail huddled together. Gustav was in the middle with water cans on each side. The machine-gun ammunition were close by.

We sat there in silence thinking about the message that army intelligence had sent through the lines that morning. We thought about what seemed to be a hopeless situation. I looked around to see the other men in our unit, but it was too dark to see them.

"Come on," someone whispered. "Let's go."

I turned my head quickly. My mouth flew open. At the same time Albert turned his head in my direction. Gustav had made the suggestion. Without any further word, he stood up. Immediately Albert and I joined him. We were open to any suggestion.

"Get your water cans," Gustav whispered.

We all picked up our cans and left the machine gun and ammunition behind. Gustav led the way. Quietly and deliberately, he ducked behind trees on his way down the hill. "Stay down low so they won't see us," he cautioned.

We headed south, walking a while, then sleeping a while in bushes. The hunger pangs got worse and worse. In the morning we found ourselves on a main country road. We passed a sign—"Euskirchen— 2 miles." We had gone through this town on our way north.

"Look," Albert exclaimed, "up there." He pointed up the road in front of us. In the distance we saw a group of men walking on the same road we were on and going in the same direction. They were German soldiers.

"Let's get off the road," Gustav advised. "There may be others behind us."

Using the road as a guide, we walked along and through the bushes beside the road. About an hour later we heard the tramping of a group of people.

"Sounds like soldiers," Gustav warned. "Run for cover."

The three of us darted for a big bush. The soldiers did not look to the right or left as they passed by. They looked straight ahead. It was an exhausted, discouraged-looking group. They were part of what became a vast movement in one direction—running from the advancing enemy.

We kept walking, watching out for those who would put us back in the army. All day long we followed the road. Lunchtime went by, and still we had not eaten. Gustav spotted a barn situated a short distance from the road.

"Hey, let's go over to that barn and see if we can find some food."

"Let's go," I said. "We've got to have some food. I'm starving."

"Suppose the owner will mind?" Albert asked.

"Maybe he won't be there," Gustav suggested. "It doesn't look like there's any activity going on."

No one was around, not even a dog or cat. We went inside the barn and found nothing more than a few bales of hay. We walked back outside and looked around. On one side of the barn we spotted a mound of dirt.

"We may find something in that," Albert suggested. He went over to the dirt and began digging. Gustav and I joined him.

"Look," Albert exclaimed, holding up a turnip for our inspection. I found it difficult to get excited about a turnip, even in my advanced hunger state.

Albert laid the turnip down on the grass beside the dirt and continued digging. We all dug until we had a big pile. Then I got out my pocketknife and cut a few apart. We leaned against the barn and ate the turnips until we were full. We wrapped the rest of them in a cloth to take with us.

After filling our water cans, we proceeded on our way south. That night we slept in the bushes again. Albert left us the next day. "It will be safer if we separate," he told us. "In our beat-up uniforms, anyone will know we're running from something. And three people are more noticeable than one."

"But you don't need to head toward your home until we get to Mayen. We'll be there tomorrow. Why don't you wait?" Gustav urged.

"No, I want to start in that direction now. I'm afraid we'll get caught."

We knew what happened to deserters. Life was bleak, but we wanted to live. We understood Albert's fears; still, we didn't want to admit what he felt. We wished him well as he headed northwest; we understood his hope to be reunited with his family.

At noon Gustav and I sat down under a tree beside the road. We ate some turnips. "I guess about now Albert is eating the ones he took," Gustav said.

"Guess so," I replied. "Lucky we found them. We haven't run across anything else."

"I don't know which is worse, sitting in a foxhole or dodging the army officials. I'm as hungry and tired as I was then."

"That was worse," I said confidently. "We may find help soon."

In the late afternoon Gustav and I came in sight of a farmhouse. It faced the road we were using as a traveling guide. "Do you think they would let us in for the night?" Gustav asked.

"Maybe. They're German, and we're German."

"Let's try. If they would just let us sleep on the floor, that would be better than the bushes."

"It sure would."

We walked down the long gravel driveway to the front yard. I led the way to the front door and knocked a couple of times. In a minute an old woman answered the knock. She looked surprised and shocked.

"What are you doing here?" she asked.

"We're on our way home," I said. "But we have a long way to go."

She did not respond to my words but just stared at me with a look of terror in her eyes.

"Could we come in?" I asked in desperation. "We're very tired and hungry."

"What is it?" an old man asked. "What do they want?" The old man stood behind his wife.

She turned to talk to him. "They want to come in and rest." They gave each other a knowing look.

"No . . . no, we can't do that," he told us.

"Why? Why?" I pleaded, "We're just kids. We won't hurt you. And we'll leave in the morning."

"If we let German soldiers in, and the enemy comes, they will hurt us."

"But we're your own people. Can't you understand that?"

The old woman turned to her husband again; a look of compassion filled her face. But he would not give in. He broke the gaze and turned to us. "No, no, we can't help you. You must go!"

"Could we have something to eat?" Gustav asked. "We don't even have to come inside. We could travel on and eat it along the way."

"No. Go on! Go on!" the old man insisted. "They may come by anytime. Go on!" He waved his arms to shoo us away and shut the door in our faces.

We stood facing the closed door for a minute, stunned and dismayed. Knowing we had no other choice, we turned and walked down the long driveway to the main road. We had been deserted by our own people—a typical sign of a nation in defeat.

As we continued south, the Rhine River became our guide, replacing the road. Occasionally we passed a sign that pointed in the direction of a town.

We walked and walked in the direction of home— at least what we thought would be home. We slept in bushes and barns, any place that afforded us shelter from the weather. Keeping in mind the experience at the farmhouse, we did not ask for permission to sleep in the barns. We would spot a barn, then slip in after dark, nestle in the warmth of the hay, and leave early the next morning. The owner had no opportunity to say no.

Near Mainz, we came to a bombed-out house. "We can stay in the cellar," Gustav said.

"Maybe there will be some food," I hoped.

There was no food, but it was a fairly comfortable place to stay, at least compared to the bushes. After a restful night's sleep we were awakened by the sound of dogs barking. Gustav and I looked at each other in terror.

"They'll catch us and turn us over to the authorities," Gustav gasped, huddling beside me in the dark corner of the cellar. "Look! They're in the doorway!"

"Be quiet! They'll hear you."

In the sunlight that trickled through the doorway we could see the two dogs clearly. They looked extremely vicious.

"What can we do?" Gustav asked.

"Just stay still. We can't do anything." For a long minute, we watched the dogs while our fears multiplied.

Then someone whistled. The dogs turned quickly and ran.

"Let's get out of here," I suggested. "They may come back."

We picked up our water cans, put on our coats, and climbed up the steps to the opening where a door had been before the bombing. A gentle breeze greeted us. The sun shone brightly; the sky was completely clear. It was a beautiful spring day, a little warmer than usual for the end of March.

We walked in the grass near the western bank of the Rhine. Not far from the house we saw a bundle.

"It's a knapsack," Gustav exclaimed. "I hope there's something in it." He ran to check. I was close behind him.

Gustav loosened the string that held the knapsack shut; he reached inside and lifted a can out. "Potted meat. That's great!" He lifted another can out. "Green beans. We're in luck." There were several cans in the sack.

With my knife I opened the cans, and we sat down to a breakfast of potted meat and green beans. "We'll have enough for several meals," Gustav said with relief evident in his voice.

We were afraid to go into any town or village where many people were gathered. But as we traveled, we asked the few people we met where the enemy was. We didn't want *anyone* to catch us. We were convinced the Americans were ruthless bombers. We knew that the Russians would send us to Siberia and that the French would send us to Africa.

We didn't want to be POWs; nor did we want to be prosecuted by our own people. We knew about the rebellion of 1944 when the army generals rose up against Hitler—at that time even a general field marshal was executed for his part in the plot. Many times during my journey to our hunting lodge, I pictured myself against a wall, waiting for someone to pull the trigger.

At Mainz we crossed the Rhine. We had been on the road for two weeks. For the noon meal we ate the last cans of potted meat and green beans.

"I guess I'll head east toward Frankfurt now," Gustav announced after the meal. "That's on the way home."

"I'm going to keep traveling south for a while and then turn east and head toward our hunting lodge in Austria," I told him. "Vati said to go there if anything happened. I'm not sure anyone will be there, though."

I felt deep sadness when Gustav and I parted. We had become real buddies during the two weeks of traveling together. We had come to depend upon each other. Now I was alone, and loneliness wasn't a good feeling. But there was no other way.

That evening I came to a restaurant. I walked inside and sat down at the counter. A waiter with a pleasant-looking face and a pleasant manner brought me a menu.

"I'm a soldier," I told him when he came to take my order. "I need something to eat, but I have no money."

He looked at my tattered clothing. Then he looked at my face. "You look like you could use a good meal. Number 2 is good. How does that sound to you?"

I glanced down at the menu but didn't read what was under the number. "That will be fine," I said. Anything would be fine!

The man's wife brought the plate of food to me. It was the biggest and best-looking meal I had eaten in a long time. She set a big glass of milk in front of my plate.

"Thank you; thank you," I said.

"Do you have a place to stay tonight?" the woman asked me after I had finished eating.

"No, I don't," I replied. "I'm on my way to Austria."

"You can stay with us," she offered. "We have an extra bed." That was the only time on the trip that I slept in a bed. And I took my first bath in weeks.

The next morning the kind couple fed me a hearty breakfast. Unlike the old couple at the farm, they were not afraid to help a German soldier.

"Do you want to stay another night?" the woman asked after breakfast. "You still look tired."

"No. I must keep moving. I'm anxious to get to Austria. Thanks, anyway. You both have been so kind."

Before I finished eating, the man came up to the counter and stood in front of me with a sack in his hand. "Take this food with you," he said, smiling.

"Thank you, sir. I'll never forget your kindness."

I told them both good-bye and went on my way. I still looked terrible in my ragged and dirty clothes, but I was clean and full and grateful.

I kept moving, sleeping in the bushes, searching for food, dodging the enemy. The days passed slowly as I traveled alone with no one to talk to, no one to help pass the time, no one to encourage me. At Freiburg I turned east toward the Lake of Constance. In a village near the lake I asked a farmer for directions.

"How do I get to Reutte, Austria?"

Before he answered, he looked at my uniform. "Oh, you've come home from the war," he observed.

"Yes," I said softly, not knowing whether to stay or run.

"You need to get that uniform off. Let me see what I can find."

I stayed outside while the man went into his house. I felt uneasy. How did I know he could be trusted? But I really had no choice.

The man came back with a civilian jacket across his

arm. "Here, try this," he said, handing the jacket to me.

I took off the heavy army regulation overcoat that I had been wearing since I left the army. I put on the jacket; it fit all right.

"That looks fine," the man said. "It isn't good to have a uniform on these days. The Allied forces are moving in."

I thanked the man and went on my way, following his directions to Austria. A few miles north of the Austrian border I saw the Allied forces, but they did not see me. Finally I came to the sign I longed desperately to see: Entering Austria, Leaving Bavaria.

I've finally made it, I thought. Soon I would be in Reutte. My four-week journey was about to end. Compared to how far I had come, the hunting lodge was a very short distance away. When I reached Reutte, there would be only twenty-five miles left on my journey.

I sneaked into Reutte, trying not to attract any attention. I wanted to go on through the town and start up the mountain road to Bach, where our lodge was located.

As I walked down the main street of the town, I saw several German officers standing on the street corner. Their backs were turned to me. I looked for a place to hide. Then I remembered that I did not have on an army uniform anymore. They would assume that I was an Austrian teenage boy.

I came closer to the group. The uniforms were familiar. They were just like the one my father had had on the last time I had seen him.

Suddenly a military motorcyclist came from one of the side streets and approached the officers. "Have the Allies broken through?" he asked.

One officer replied quickly. "As long as we're standing here, they're not coming in. You better tell them that." The group roared with laughter.

I recognized the voice. "That's Vati," I whispered.

"Vati!" I ran to the group. As I came near, one of the men turned in my direction.

He looked surprised and cautious. "What do you want?" he said sternly.

Before I could say anything, my father and the other officers turned around.

"Traugott!" Vati exclaimed. "What are you doing?" He came closer to me and put his arm around my shoulder. "Where have you been?"

"I've just come on home," I said quietly.

The other men respected our privacy. They turned around and continued their conversation. Surely they knew we had been separated for some time.

I gazed into my father's face as he explained that he had come home from Yugoslavia because of sickness. His comments were brief. He looked so tired. His fencing scar was more prominent than ever. His skin was a funny yellow color. I had never seen him in such a pitiful condition.

I gave no further explanation than "I've just come home." And he asked for no more.

"Your mother and sister are at the lodge," he told me. "A truck is coming to take us there in an hour." He told me that the truck would stop at a location several blocks away.

I wanted him to continue talking to his friends. "I'll meet you down there," I said. I walked on down to the pickup spot to wait. A renewed vigor filled my body and soul. I was extremely happy. It was hard to believe that my family would be together again. For the first time since I had deserted, I felt safe.

The truck was on time to pick us up. There were several others returning to Bach with us. My father rode in the front with the driver, and I rode in back. At Bach the driver let us off at the village store. We walked to our hunting lodge.

Evidently Mutti saw us coming up the street because she and Maria came running to us.

"Oh, Traugott," Mutti sobbed. "I've been so worried about you. Where have you been?"

"In the West, but I've come home for good," I replied.

She hugged me for several minutes. And to my surprise, Maria hugged me, too. Mutti and Vati embraced and kissed.

"Let's go on in," Mutti said. "Supper is almost ready."

We walked into the house and sat down in the living room. After a few words, we went to our rooms to clean up. My bed from Augsburg was in my room. I didn't know that it had been saved. Seeing it gave me a secure feeling.

"I'm so happy we can be together," Vati sighed as we sat down to eat. He repeated the words several times during the evening. Still, he was so withdrawn, so preoccupied. He was not the powerful man he had once been.

We didn't talk about the war much, but we did listen to the radio. As usual, the news reports began with the familiar tune—"We are driving; we are driving . . . ." And as usual, the announcer stated that we were winning the war. Prisoners were taken; tanks were destroyed. The Allied forces were being driven out of our homeland.

"Shut it off," Vati blurted out in the middle of the announcements. "They don't believe what they're saying themselves."

Mutti leaned over the end of the sofa and turned it off. We sat in silence for a few moments. I couldn't believe what I had just heard. Vati had finally admitted what we all feared.

We went to our rooms early. In their room Mutti and Vati talked about the war situation. "I feel like a man sitting in a car that's going down a hill," my father told her as they talked. "But it's too late to get out."

Just before he retired for the evening, Vati stuck his head in my bedroom door. "Traugott, we'll go hunting in the morning and forget about the war."

"Great," I said, hoping he would let me shoot.

The dead tone in my father's voice bothered me. The war had taken so much from him.

5
April 28, 1945

April 28, 1945, was the day Benito Mussolini, the Italian dictator, was killed. That day Vati and I rose before dawn to go hunting. Mutti was up before us, preparing breakfast.

"Good morning, Mutti," I said as I walked to her at the stove and kissed her on the cheek.

She put her arm around my shoulder. "Good morning, Traugott. Did you sleep well?" I detected a sad look in her eyes. She forced a smile, but her eyes did not match the smile.

"Yes, Mutti," I replied. "A real bed felt great. It's so nice to be home."

I sat down at the table and watched her work—as I had watched Berta many times. Mutti had rarely cooked before the evacuation.

In a few minutes Mutti had the food on the table. For wartime it was a feast—several kinds of bread, jams, and coffee. There had been few meals like this lately.

"Go tell Vati that breakfast is ready."

I went upstairs to Vati's bedroom and knocked on the door lightly. I didn't want to wake Maria.

"Yes, what is it?"

"Time to eat, Vati."

"All right. I'll be right there."

Shortly Vati came down the stairs and into the kitchen. He walked over to Mutti, who was getting some butter out of the refrigerator.

"Hi, darling," he said affectionately.

"Hi, darling," she replied with an affectionate smile.

They embraced and kissed, then joined me at the table. I was glad we were together again. I had missed them both so much.

"Are you ready to help me get a deer, Traugott?" Vati asked.

"Sure," I replied. I wished he would let me shoot, but I knew what the answer would be—"You're too young to shoot."

We took our time eating. "It's good to be together," Vati repeated more than once. We talked about the good times at the lodge in days past, climbing the mountains, hunting, playing in the snow. I thought about the war, too.

"Did your work go well in Yugoslavia, Vati?" I had never asked him about the war before, but I had been there myself now.

"So, so. We had some victories," he said dryly. He mentioned possibilities for the future in that area. His words were so vague, so void of enthusiasm; they hardly made sense. I could tell he didn't want to talk about the war, so I asked no more. He looked tired and sick.

Vati rose from the table. "We better get going, Traugott. You get the guns and ammunition while I get my jacket and boots on."

He walked up to his and Mutti's bedroom while I finished eating my last piece of bread. "You make good breakfasts, Mutti," I said as I got up from the table.

"I'm glad you . . ." Her reply was interrupted by a loud *thump, thump, thump* at the front door.

"Who can that be at this time of the morning?" Mutti questioned. "Go see."

The knock scared me, but I didn't know why. Slowly I opened the door. I saw the uniform first—the SS uniform. Then I looked at the man. He was a little younger than my father. A woman stood by his side, smiling. I knew the faces.

"Hello, General Juers," I said respectfully. "Hello, Mrs. Juers."

Heino Juers, our neighbor in Augsburg, had been instrumental in getting my father to go back into the military. In Augsburg he had been a colonel; the white lapels on his jacket identified his current rank. Over his uniform he wore a camouflaged jacket. Apparently he was ready for battle.

"Is the doctor here?" he asked.

"Yes, I'll get him. Won't you come in?"

He and Mrs. Juers stepped inside the door. The general closed the door behind them. And I rushed to Vati's bedroom. "General Juers is here," I said excitedly.

He looked surprised. "Oh? Get my uniform jacket in the closet."

I went to the closet and found his jacket. He took off his hunting jacket and replaced it with the proper dress. He would not appear before a superior officer out of uniform.

I followed him as he walked down the stairs to greet the general. They both raised their right arms to salute. "Heil Hitler," they said, almost in unison.

"Come to the living room and sit down," Vati said, motioning in that direction. Then he turned to me. "Traugott, tell Mutti that Mrs. Juers is here."

Like my father, my mother appeared surprised when I told her the general and his wife had come. She went into the living room to greet them; and for a few minutes, they engaged in small talk. Then General Juers announced the purpose of his visit—he wanted some strategy advice.

My mother responded immediately. "Let's go to the back, Mrs. Juers. We have nothing to say about military matters. Let me put your things in here." She pointed to the spare room downstairs.

Mrs. Juers took off her coat and handed it and her bag to Mutti. I stayed in the living room with the men, hoping Vati would not ask me to leave.

The general laid a map on the table near the side window, where the morning sun provided a good light. They both stood in front of the map examining it. "Here we are," the general said, pointing to the valley where our hunting lodge was located. "We must keep the enemy from advancing into this area."

"How do you plan to stop their advance?" Vati asked.

"We could mass our troops along this line," he said, drawing a line to the north of us. The line bordered an area approximately fifty miles wide, running east and west.

"But look here," Vati said. "They could block off that pass and trap you. And to the east and west they could trap you, too."

"They wouldn't get that far if we have some artillery support," the general argued.

"Could we get that support?" Vati asked with skepticism in his voice.

"I'm not sure. But I still think we can manage without it if we have to."

"We don't have a chance," my father sighed. "Our supplies are too low."

The general ignored objection after objection. He was determined to defend the valley. By midmorning my father quit objecting and began to help him map out his strategy. At noon they stopped long enough to eat a sandwich.

Around two o'clock, two cars drove up and parked in front of the lodge. A corporal got out of one car and came to the door. I answered the knock. "Would you tell General Juers that his cars are here?"

"Yes, I will," I said. "I'll get him."

I walked over to the table where the two men were working. "Excuse me, General Juers . . . ."

"Yes?"

"Your cars are here."

He walked to the door and greeted the corporal, then looked at his watch. "It *is* time to go," he said. "I'll be there in a minute." The corporal turned and walked back to the cars. The general shut the door, walked over to the table, and hurriedly folded the map and gathered up his notes.

"I must go now," he announced. "I will meet my unit in the village at two-thirty." He turned to me. "Would you tell Mrs. Juers that it is time to go?"

I went to the kitchen and gave Mrs. Juers the message. "Let me wrap up some of these cookies for you to take, Mrs. Juers," my mother offered. "You'll probably eat late, and they'll make a nice snack."

"I'd love to have them. That's so thoughtful of you; they are Heino's favorite. Let me get my things while you wrap them." She went to the spare room to get her coat and bag. Mutti handed her the cookies when she returned to the kitchen. She thanked her and put them in her bag. They both walked to the living room to join the men.

"Did you two have a nice visit?" Vati asked.

"Yes," they said together, smiling.

"It was nice to be together again," Mutti added. "We'll walk you to the car."

Vati walked to the door and opened it, and they all went outside. I followed them and stood in the doorway as the four went down the steps to the front lawn. When they were about halfway to the cars, Mrs. Juers waved to her son, who was driving the first car. He waved back and smiled.

The general felt his jacket pockets, apparently trying to find something. "Doctor," he asked, "do you have some cigarettes? I seem to be out."

"Certainly," Vati replied. "Mutti, would you get some cigarettes for the general, please? They're on the mantle above the fireplace."

"I'd be happy to." She turned and walked toward the lodge. She looked up and saw me but was too close to bother having me get the cigarettes. While the other three waited in the center of the lawn, she went on past me to the fireplace. I stayed in the doorway.

Suddenly the loud staccato sound of a submachine gun pierced the air like a garbled scream. "ta-ta-ta-ta-ta." The sound tore through the sunny afternoon furiously, paused, then repeated. The general fell backward.

The general's wife screamed. "Help! Help! I've been hit." She grabbed her side and ran stumbling into the lodge. Mutti ran to her and helped her to the couch.

While I watched, horrified, my father pitched forward to the ground onto his face. The tearing rattle of machine-gun fire continued, but my shock at seeing my father fall made me ignore the bullets. I ran to his side even while the bullets tore at the ground and cars around me. I fell down beside him and turned him over. "Vati, Vati," I cried.

He was still, completely limp. His eyes were wide open; blood seeped from the side of his mouth and ran into the deep fencing scar on his chin. I looked down to his stomach. "Oh, no," I gasped. The bullets had exploded inside his body, tearing his stomach and abdomen completely open. I knew about that type of bullet.

My mind rejected what I saw. I muttered and screamed over and over, "No, no, no. It can't be. It can't be." With desperate agony, I pulled his coat over the wound in a foolish and futile gesture to stop the blood from pouring out. The fiery bullets stopped suddenly. I glanced over at the general. He lay very still. Unable to move, I sat on the ground beside my father.

The general's son jumped out of his car and ran to his father.

"He's dead," I screamed. "He's dead. He's dead." Dazed, I didn't know which man I was talking about, my father or the general. It didn't matter.

Ignoring me, he checked his father and then ran to the lodge. A moment later he came out the door, carrying his mother in his arms. She was still alive but in great pain.

"I hope they can save her," I said. He did not respond. He laid her in the car and raced away. A few hours later his mother died in the hospital. The son did not return to the lodge.

I walked into the lodge, my shoulders stooped in

disbelief. Mutti and Maria met me in the doorway, unaware of the extent of the tragedy.

"Vati is dead," I blurted out in response to their questioning looks.

"Oh, no," Mutti cried. She clasped her breast as if she were going to faint. Maria screamed and burst into tears.

I took Mutti in my arms. She sobbed and sobbed. Maria put her arms around us both, closing us in a circle of agony. I was too numb to cry. We stood there in the doorway for several minutes.

"Let's sit down," Mutti suggested solemnly, pointing to the living room.

"What will we do now?" Maria asked through her tears. "What will we do?"

"I don't know," I said quietly. "It all seems so unreal, like a bad dream."

"We were so happy yesterday," Maria sobbed. "And now. . . ." She put her head in her hands and continued sobbing.

Real shock set in. The joy of yesterday's reunion was something of the distant past. "Did we really get back together?" I asked myself. "Maybe none of this happened."

A little later we heard voices outside. I went to the window to see who it was.

"It's some German soldiers," I observed. "What do they want?" About ten of them were in the group, along with two officers.

"What are they here for?" Maria asked.

"Just looking, I guess. Maybe they will help us bury Vati and the general."

The soldiers surveyed the bloody scene, shaking their heads. Two or three walked around the driveway to the back of the lodge. I stepped outside.

One officer with four or five soldiers marched up to my father. The officer raised his arm to salute. "You died for the Führer," he said confidently. I cringed. Ceremoniously, he called all of the soldiers to the general and repeated the same words.

I remembered my father's words when he looked at our home in Augsburg after the bombing. "This is the price we have to pay."

Is *this the price we have to pay?* I wondered. I had never seen a loved one die before. And that loved one was my idol. *Why did I have to pay such a price?* I asked silently.

When the rest of the group came back to the front yard, one officer motioned for them to leave. "We will join our unit in the village," he said.

I ran to the officer. "Who will bury them?" I shouted frantically.

The soldiers stared at me blankly. "We must move on," the officer said.

"But they're SS officers. They served our country for many years."

No one responded to my plea. On signal, they all left as quickly as they had appeared.

Mutti came to the door and looked at the bloody scene once more. "We must move them," she said somberly.

"I'll do it, Mutti. Just leave the front door open, and go get some rest."

I walked over to my father's body. Standing above his head, I put a hand under each armpit. By then he was covered with blood. I felt it run across my fingers. Fighting a growing nausea, I dragged him slowly to the front steps, then up the steps to the door. His legs left a trail of blood as I dragged him to the front bedroom.

I stopped in front of the bedroom door and laid my daddy down while I pushed the door open. The room was nearly empty; we had no bed for it. I laid him on his back in the center of the room. As I pulled his jacket together, I noticed the Iron Cross medal pinned below the upper pocket. I knelt down beside him, unfastened the medal, and took it off. Each movement accented the painful reality of death. On his left hand he wore the family seal ring. As I slowly and deliberately removed it, a lump formed in my throat. I wanted to cry, but the tears would not come. This last action was so final. An only child, Vati had lost his father when he was nine years old. Now, at fifteen, I, too, had lost my father. I was the only Vogel left.

I looked at his face again. His eyes still were open, so I closed them. The deep fencing scar looked grotesque with drying blood caked in the cavity. I found a washcloth and cleaned his face. In death he looked more stern, more serious than ever—more stern than he actually was. I turned, walked out of the room, and shut the door behind me. My stomach began to ache. Sweat poured from my brow.

I went to the bathroom to wash my hands. Glancing into the mirror, I saw that my clothes were covered with blood, my father's blood. A dull pain hit the base of my back.

It was getting dark, but my work was not over. There was another body to move. I tried not to feel anymore as I dragged the general's body to the back of the house and put him in the barn. But the feelings emerged—feelings of resentment. Juers had talked my father into rejoining the military, I was sure. At fifty-five years of age, Vati had been exempt. *If only my father had never met you,* I thought as I closed the barn door. *Maybe he would be alive now.* Many times in later years that thought surfaced. *If only Vati had never met Heino Juers.*

I dismissed the feeling and went into the lodge. Mutti and Maria had gone to their rooms. I got a glass of milk and walked to my room, feeling so desolate, so alone, empty, helpless. My world was shattered. The ecstatic joy of being home together was completely erased, forgotten, in such a short time.

As I drank the milk, I began to consider what the tragedy meant for my family's future. A reality that had been in the back of my mind hit me. I saw it in the faces of the people in the village but ignored the evidence. Vati alluded to the possibility at our first meal together. He knew much more than I did about the total situation. All the experiences of the past weeks dovetailed into one realization: It was dangerous to be what we were—an SS family, *Gottgläubig*, Hitler's protection squad.

"I'll get rid of the evidence," I decided. I went to my mother's bedroom and knocked on the door. "Mutti, are you awake?"

"Yes, come in," she said weakly. I opened the door to find her sitting in a chair beside the bed. In the dim light of the lamp beside her, I could see that her eyes were red and swollen.

"I need to get Vati's military clothes."

"Turn on the overhead light so you can see better." She did not ask me to explain. She knew why I wanted them. I searched the closet carefully. First I found his dress uniform, then his camouflage jacket, his extra work uniform, his shirts, his ties—everything connected with an SS officer.

I took the clothes to my room, laid them on the bed, and went outside to get some big rocks. I brought the rocks in, placed them on top of the clothes, and tied the clothes securely around them, forming a bundle. In the darkness I trudged across the valley in front of the lodge, then down to the river, and threw in the bundle.

The bundle made a deep splash. It was too dark to watch it sink, but I could tell by the sound that the clothes were out of sight, on their way down the river. I breathed a sigh of relief.

It was late when I finally fell into bed, but I couldn't sleep. Over and over the terrible death scene passed before my eyes. I heard the bullets; I saw the scar, the Iron Cross, the ring, the looks of agony.

Early the next day the local Austrian police came to take notes on what had happened. They asked for someone to come outside. Since Mutti and Maria did not want to talk to them, I went out. When I told the policemen about the general's wife, one of them said, "Oh, they shot a civilian?" A few minutes later, when they were walking around the lodge, presumably looking for evidence, I overheard the policeman remark to his partner, "They shouldn't have shot the civilian. They can be prosecuted for that." I didn't see any difference. They had murdered my father—and the general, too. Vati and General Juers had been human beings as surely as the civilian.

When the two men left, I went to the village to find someone to help me. On the way, one of my father's hunting companions stopped to talk with me.

"I heard about the killing. Do you know who did it?" he asked.

"I have no idea."

"Did you know that Austrian guerillas are in the hills behind your lodge?"

"No, I didn't. I just got here the day before yesterday."

"There are two from our neighborhood up there." He named them and pointed to their homes. I knew who they were.

"Do you think they had any part in it?"

He shrugged his shoulders. "Who knows?"

Some months later when the people were not so scared, the names of the two guerillas came up in conversations in the village. The people let us know who the murderers were.

I was too tired to pursue the subject anymore then. "I've got to go," I said. "I'm going to the village to get someone to help me bury my father and the general."

He offered no help.

I went to the village priest first. A man of God would help me, I was sure. He was standing in front of the church building talking to a man when I walked up. I waited for them to finish their conversation. He greeted me but did not seem to recognize me.

"Did you hear about my father?" I asked.

A look of recognition flashed across his face. "Oh, you are the young Vogel," he said. "Yes. Everyone knows. I know you have suffered greatly."

"Will you help me bury him?"

He answered quickly. "I just can't do that."

"Why?"

"He was a godless man," he replied abruptly. "They were both godless men."

"But you knew my father. He was a good man," I argued.

He softened a little. "I would have to get permission from my superiors."

"How long would that take?" I asked, sensing that he was merely making excuses.

"Several days," he replied.

"But that is too long. I need to bury him today."

"I'm sorry," he said quietly. "I can't help you."

I was too upset to say anymore. "A man of God," I muttered under my breath as I walked away. "A man of God. I can't believe it."

On down to the village store, I walked. Along the way a few people stopped to say a word, but no one would help. No one wanted to be connected with SS officers.

I went to one of the town officials and asked him for help. "Throw them in the river," he laughed sarcastically. "They're just Germans." The pain went deep. Hate was so big, so evident, so hard for a teenage boy to understand or face.

In desperation I went back to the priest. "I've got to bury them somewhere. No one will help me. Can't you do something?" I pleaded.

He told me about a plot in the cemetery that I could use. That was the most help he could give. I could tell he was anxious for me to leave. I thanked him and went home for a shovel to dig the graves.

The digging was slow because the ground was still hard from the winter snows. I decided to dig a double grave. As I worked, sweat poured from my brow; my hands and arms began to ache. But I couldn't quit. There was no one else to do it.

I heard steps behind me. I turned quickly.

"You need some help?" the man asked.

I couldn't believe my ears or eyes. It was Johann, the hermit. Nobody liked him because he was strange looking. And everybody thought his mind was weak.

"Oh, yes, please," I sighed.

He had a shovel in his hand, prepared to work. The two of us dug until we had a grave of reasonable depth.

"Now we need to get some boards for the coffins," I told him.

"I've got some," he offered. "They're not too fancy, though."

"They'll be fine, I'm sure."

We walked to his home, a dilapidated cabin badly in need of repair. It had not been painted in years. Behind the cabin we found some boards—not very good, as Johann had said, but they would do.

"Let's take them to my place. We have some boards by the barn," I said.

He picked up a hammer and a container with nails. I carried the boards. We walked on up the road to our lodge, saying very little.

As I had remembered, there were some boards beside the barn, a little warped but usable. We arranged the boards in two piles—one for each coffin. I nailed the boards together for Vati's coffin; Johann constructed the coffin for the general. When we finished we put the coffins by the back door, near the barn.

"We need to get the bodies now," I said solemnly. I cringed at the thought of seeing the bodies again. "Let's get the general first," I suggested. "He's in the barn."

Johann picked up the general's feet. I put my hands under his arms, and we carried the body to the coffin.

"They sure shot him up," Johann remarked.

"Yeah," I said. "Cold-blooded murder." We nailed the top on.

"Let's go get my father. He's in the house."

We went in the back door and through the kitchen,

where Mutti was working. She greeted Johann. "This way, Johann," I said, pointing in the direction of the bedroom.

Slowly I opened the bedroom door where my father lay. He looked worse than the general, but Johann said nothing when we picked him up. Again, he took the legs; I put my hands under Vati's arms; and we carried him to the coffin. I sat down to get my breath while Johann nailed on the top.

The horrible death scene came to mind once more. The shots, screams, blood, panic, death—it all came back. I hated the murderers. *I'll get them,* I vowed silently.

"We need some markers," I told Johann. "But there's no time for that now. I'll get them later."

Fifteen years later I did get a marker. In 1960 I wrote to Chancellor Gorbach, head of the Austrian government, requesting permission to put a plaque on Vati's grave. Both the general and my father had been moved to a military cemetery for German soldiers on the outskirts of Reutte, Austria, so special permission was necessary to change anything. The Chancellor graciously granted permission and wrote a letter telling me that he had been imprisoned at Dachau. Evidently he had opposed the annexation of Austria to Germany in 1938. I sent the plaque to Austria, and Mr. Gorbach arranged for it to be put on the grave and even sent pictures to me. Vati's steel helmet was placed on top of the marker.

Each year, on the anniversary of the deaths of my father and the general, former SS officers adorn the double grave with a beautiful wreath. The wreath, called "A Sprig of Faithfulness," is a reminder of the imprint on the sword carried by SS officers—MY HONOR IS FAITHFULNESS.

"How will we get them to the cemetery?" I asked. "We can't carry them that far."

"Erwin has a cart. Maybe he will let us use it." He pointed to a house down the block.

"You go; he probably won't give it to me."

He understood. I followed him to the front yard and watched him walk down the street. His trousers were baggy; his coat was greasy and worn. His shoes were crusty. He did look strange, but I had discovered his kindness. "How would I ever have done it alone?" I whispered. The possibility overwhelmed me. I was so exhausted emotionally and physically—and there was still more to do.

"Are you about finished, Traugott?" Mutti called from the front door.

I walked over to her. "Not too much longer, Mutti. Johann has gone for a cart."

"We'll get dressed then."

Shortly Johann returned with the horse-drawn cart. He guided it up the driveway that went behind the lodge, and we lifted the coffins onto the cart. There was just enough room for them.

Mutti and Maria came out of the lodge. Mutti looked so haggard, so tired, so sad, so deserted. She had lost another husband before his time. She never forgave God for taking two husbands from her.

Mutti, Maria, and I walked behind the cart, while Johann led the horse. Down the driveway to the street we went. I saw a neighbor pull back the curtains to see us. On down the street, the same thing happened again . . . and again. All along the way people stared, but no one spoke. I tried to look straight ahead, but that was impossible. I wanted to see the faces, to read the thoughts.

One block gone; two, three, four. Finally we had gone the long mile and were at the entrance to the cemetery. Johann turned in and proceeded to the gravesite.

We lifted the coffins out of the cart and placed them beside the double grave. The three of us stood by the coffins. Johann moved back. Mutti and Maria sobbed bitterly. I tried to comfort them.

After a few minutes I motioned to Johann. "Let's lower the coffins." Mutti and Maria stepped back toward the cart while we lowered the coffins into the grave and shoveled dirt over them.

That final action tore me apart. Suddenly I fell down beside the grave. "Why? Why?" I whispered in agony. But I couldn't cry; I hurt too much. Some time later, as I walked in the woods, the tears did come. Alone, out of the sight and hearing of everyone, I let my emotions go. I cried and cried, deeply aware of my great loss. But at the gravesite the tears would not come.

I felt an arm around my shoulder. "We can't do anymore now," Mutti said tenderly. I looked up into her eyes. Tears were streaming down her cheeks. "Let's go home, Traugott."

Slowly I got up. Johann turned the cart around. I looked back at the unmarked grave.

As Johann guided the horse in front of us we passed the same people we had seen on the way to the cemetery. We endured the same stares. As we approached the lodge, I thanked Johann for all his help. Words were not adequate to express my gratitude.

Silently the three of us walked up the driveway with our private thoughts. I hated everyone who was responsible for this act—Americans, Russians, French, British, and most of all, the men who fired the shots that killed Vati. I was determined to get even with the killers one day. Often during the time before we were sent back to Germany, my mother tried to temper my hate. "There are good and bad ones everywhere," she told me many times when my hostility was evident. She learned to live with her sorrow and disappointment.

That night as I lay in bed, I recalled conversations with my father. I remembered that once when I cleaned his jackboots, I couldn't get the spurs back on. "You'll never make an officer," he told me jokingly. I *was* going to be an officer. I was going to be just like him. The tragedy shattered but did not erase my dream.

Eight days later, May 7, 1945, Germany officially

surrendered to the Western Allies. On May 9, Russian troops marched into Berlin. I could not even guess what the future held for me. I'm not sure I wanted to know.

6
The SS Stigma

The year 1945 was an extremely difficult one for my mother. Her appearance reflected the strain as the lines in her face deepened, and a wide gray streak suddenly appeared in her hair. Within six months she experienced more tragedies than most people endure in a lifetime.

Vati's murder was the first family tragedy that Mutti knew about, but three other family members had died in that year—her mother, brother, and sister-in-law. She did not receive the news of their deaths until some time after the war ended. In March of 1945, Grandmother Ratazzi died in her home in Frankfurt. Because it was not possible to contact family members, some of the nurses who worked at a hospital near her home took care of the funeral arrangements.

Soon after receiving the news of her mother's death, Mutti learned that her brother who had chosen to serve the Germans was dead. It was a crushing blow. Life was senseless. "I hate the day I came to Europe," she blurted out when she received the sad news. "All I've seen here is fighting and suffering." Such outbursts were rare; she was a strong woman.

Mutti found little comfort for her sorrow. She had no relatives in Austria; friends were almost nonexistent; and Austria was an extremely unpleasant place for Germans to live. Wherever we went we sensed a deep resentment toward us. In derision the Austrians tagged us "people from the old country." And we had to stay there and take what they dished out because Germans were not free to move about.

Since the Allied forces occupied the land, we could return to Germany only when they gave the signal.

Even though the Allies occupied the land, the Austrian guerrillas exerted a powerful influence in the country. And they had a special hatred for "people from the old country." One afternoon two guerrillas came to see us.

"Knock . . . knock . . . knock." The strokes were firm and loud.

Mutti responded to the sound.

"H-h-hello," she said, betraying a nervousness. The garb of the men revealed that they were part of a powerful group of guerrillas.

"What . . ."

"We need some items," one of the guerrillas demanded, interrupting her.

She looked startled, then dismayed. "We have so little for ourselves," she insisted.

The two guerrillas pushed the door on open, stepped inside, and looked around as we stood by helplessly. Since they were members of the Austrian underground, no one stood up to them—and lived to tell about it.

"This way," the leader said, pointing toward the dining room. They walked past Mutti and opened the china closet.

"This looks good!" the leader exclaimed. "Let's take this set."

While Mutti and Maria sat in the living room and I stood in the doorway watching, the two men removed a silver service from the closet. As they carried the items to their truck, they looked around at the furniture in the living room. The beautiful Oriental rug caught their eye.

"Very nice," one of them said.

A few days later they returned and demanded the rug. Again we stood by helplessly. With the rug they took a precious memory of my childhood. It was one of Vati's prized possessions.

After several other trips by the guerrillas to our door demanding valuable silks and linens, Mutti resolved, "This has got to stop. We won't have anything left. They're ruthless! They won't ever stop."

One evening the three of us sat in the living room considering our situation.

"Why do they do it?" I asked.

"They hate us, Traugott," Mutti replied.

"I know. Everybody hates us. And what have we done?"

"We haven't done anything to them," Maria answered. "We haven't done anything to deserve such treatment." There were tears in her eyes.

"They blame all Germans for Hitler," Mutti explained.

"That's not fair," I said. "That's not fair. They're as bad as Hitler."

"Talking this way won't solve our problem," Mutti advised. She got up from the sofa, walked to the window, and stood there for a few minutes looking out.

"What are you looking at, Mutti?" Maria asked. "Are they coming again?"

"No, I'm just thinking." She turned to me. "Traugott, I've heard them talking at the store. They say the Americans are in Holzgau. They may help us."

"Those ruthless bombers help us!" I exclaimed.

"Yes. They may be fair. There are good ones and bad ones everywhere."

"They won't help us," I argued. "No one will."

"They may. Go on down there first thing in the morning and find out."

"All right, but it probably won't help."

Early the next morning, I walked the short distance to Holzgau and found the American headquarters. "The Austrian guerrillas are plundering our home," I told one of the guards.

The guard was surprised that I could speak English. "How do you happen to speak English?" he asked.

"I learned some in school, and my mother speaks English. She was an Australian citizen before the war."

"Come this way," he said. He led me to an officer.

I told the officer that the guerrillas were plundering our home and that we could do nothing to stop them. He listened to my story and assured me that he would try to help me.

"I'll do what I can to stop them," he said. "But they are a sneaky bunch. You go on home, and we'll be in touch."

I thanked him and went on my way, not sure that I could trust anyone, especially ones who had bombed my home. But I was wrong, for the next day an American jeep with two American soldiers in it parked in front of our house.

"Look out the window, Mutti!" I exclaimed. "They did come. The Americans are here!"

"I thought they would help us," she said.

Mutti walked out to greet the Americans. When she came back inside, she told us that the soldiers had been instructed not to talk to us. "Just stay away from them so there won't be any problem," she told Maria and me.

"I guess they think they're too good for us," I suggested.

"No, that's not it. They just want to be careful. Don't be so hard on them; they're helping us."

"We'll see," I said.

In the afternoon I went out the back door and started walking in the direction of the barn. I heard someone walking on the gravel road that ran behind the house.

"Oh, no," I whispered and ran into the house.

Mutti was in the kitchen. "Mutti," I cried. "They're here again."

"Who's here?"

"The guerrillas, the guerrillas. Come and look." I led her to the back door, but they weren't there anymore.

"They must have gone around to the front," she suggested.

We went to the kitchen to look out the window. The guerrillas had just come around the side and were headed for the front door. Suddenly they stopped. One pointed in the direction of the American jeep. They talked for a minute, then turned around and walked toward the hills behind the house. We were not bothered by them again.

On May 7, 1945, when the armistice was declared, Austria became an independent country again, thus severing all ties with Germany. Soon after the signing the Americans left our area. The French were supposed to supervise the Tirol section of Austria, where we lived. Mutti, Maria, and I began to talk about what was going to happen because of the armistice. We were hounded by a feeling we couldn't express or understand. We were waiting for something to happen—what, we didn't know.

"Will they take our lodge away from us?" Maria asked.

"We bought it before the war. It's ours," Mutti assured her.

"They hate us so much," I said. "And . . . I hate them. They killed Vati and plundered our home."

"There are good and bad ones everywhere," Mutti said. "Try to remember that."

"Yes, Johann is kind," I said softly. "There's one good Austrian."

While we waited for something to happen, I roamed in the forest a lot. I had no job to occupy my time and few friends. And I wasn't sure about those few I claimed as friends. Life was so aimless.

One thing I did know for sure. I had many enemies. Often I went bike riding. One day as I went down a hill, I felt some objects hit the spokes of my bicycle. The wheel turned suddenly, and I went tumbling down the hill. I was skinned all over.

"Those dirty bums! I hate them!" I yelled, as I got up and brushed myself off. *If Vati were here,* I thought, *they wouldn't do this.*

Suddenly I heard someone laughing. I stood still, trying to determine where the sound was coming from. It was coming from a house at the top of the hill.

I'm not surprised, I thought. *They hate us. Everybody hates Germans. And I hate them. Oooooh, I hate them! They killed Vati.*

I climbed on my bicycle and pedaled home.

One unpleasant experience after another helped us to realize that our days in Austria were numbered. Every day the resentment toward Germans deepened.

"And when we leave," Mutti told us, "we can take nothing with us—except what we can carry in our arms."

My mother had a valuable jewelry collection as well as a number of fur coats. One coat was made out of costly Persian fur. We did not want to choose between these costly items and essential items we knew we must have, so we sat down one evening and made some plans.

"The Kuhlers are taking things out," Maria told us.

"How?" Mutti asked.

"Over the hills."

"Aren't there guards on the border?"

"They dodge them. They've made several trips already, and no one has caught them yet."

"We can do that, too," I suggested.

"Yes," Maria chimed in.

That's just what we decided to do. We spent the rest of the evening gathering together items to take over the hills on our first trip. We packed jewelry, fur coats, and silver settings.

Around five in the morning, Maria and I went down the valley east of our lodge. Then we began the slow climb up the mountains. Along the way up we met other Germans who were making the same trip. We simply greeted them and continued on our way. For obvious reasons, we did not congregate in large groups. Spotting us traveling by twos or threes certainly was more difficult for the border guards than seeing a crowd. The many trees and bushes afforded us instantly available hiding places. Still, there was always a chance that they would catch us.

Our loads were heavy, and the climbing was strenuous. "I'm so tired," Maria moaned at one point. "Let's rest." We had been walking and climbing for almost four hours.

"We've already stopped four times," I said. "We're almost there, anyway."

"I don't care; I want to stop."

"All right, Maria. But we would enjoy our rest a lot more if we went on across the border. There it is, up there." I pointed to a stone partially covered by the "eternal" snow at the top of the mountain.

"It looks close," she said. "But it will probably take an hour to get there."

"All right, all right," I relented.

We sat down and rested for ten or fifteen minutes. The air up that high was chilly, and there were few trees to hide us now.

"Ready?" I asked.

"Yes. Let's go," she replied.

We trudged on up the mountain. Finally we could see the imprint on the border marker. On our side was a "T," standing for Tirol. We knew a "B" was chiseled on the other side—a "B" which stood for Bavaria, a section of Germany.

"I can't wait to touch that 'B,' " I exclaimed.

"Me, too," Maria concurred.

We heard someone walking at the top of the mountain.

"The guards are coming," I whispered, looking for a hiding place. "Get behind that rock," I said, pointing to a huge rock a few steps down the mountain. We crouched down behind the rock.

"What will they do if they catch us?" Maria whispered.

"I don't really know. But you can be sure they will take our stuff."

"All these beautiful pieces of jewelry and furs?"

"Right. And even worse, we won't be able to take out anything else. They'll watch us."

We could hear the guards walking by slowly. Then they stopped, possibly to look around. We glanced down the hill.

"There's Mr. Franz," Maria gasped. "Do you think he sees the guards?"

Mr. Franz was a German who had lost an arm in the war. His wife was Austrian. The Austrians had told him that when the time came for the Germans to leave, his wife could stay, but he would have to go. He was determined to take everything with him. "I won't leave anything with those bums," he would say. He even dismantled a gas stove and carried it over the mountains.

"Why doesn't he look up?" Maria said.

"He must not see the guards." I peeked around the rock. The guards had their backs turned to us.

"Watch the guards, Maria. Tell me if they start to turn around."

She took my place at the edge of the rock. "It looks like they're going on east," she said.

I threw a rock at Mr. Franz. He looked up. I motioned up the mountain to the guards. One guard glanced down the mountain in our direction. Maria quickly pulled her head back behind the rock. Mr. Franz jumped behind a tree.

The guard said something to his companion. We couldn't understand what it was.

"We're caught," Maria cried.

"Be still. Don't say a word."

The guards stood in one spot for a few minutes. We could tell they were facing our direction. They exchanged some conversation, then started walking toward the east. We waited for a few minutes, then climbed the short distance to the top of the mountain and ran across the border.

"We're in Germany!" Maria exclaimed. "We made it!"

We stood there for a moment, gazing at the "B" chiseled on Germany's side of the stone marker. What a thrill!

"Now we have to find a place to put our stuff," I said. "Where is that ski lodge?"

"A short distance down the hill and just to the west," Maria replied.

A friend of Maria's had told her about the ski lodge. The friend had said that it was practically empty because the war had curtailed business. The owner, Mr. Meier, was happy to help fellow Germans.

When we arrived at the lodge, I made the appropriate introductions.

"Come on inside," Mr. Meier told us, "and have some coffee. You look cold and tired."

"Thank you, sir. We are very tired."

Mr. Meier looked like a typical mountain man with his ruddy complexion and thick beard. His voice was gentle and kind, though. As soon as we sat down, I made my request.

"Sure, sure," he responded. "I don't have much business these days, the war and all, you know. You can leave your things here."

"We'll come back later and take everything down to Obersdorf," I assured him. "The trip is too difficult for one day."

"I know," he said. "That will be fine. Don't worry. It will all be here when you come back."

We ate the lunch Mutti had packed for us and began our trip back home. The trek back was a breeze without the heavy load. In addition, it was downhill most of the way. We slipped across the border into Tirol without any trouble.

A couple of days later we set out on another trip up the mountain. On this trip we took a very light load, since we planned to take everything to a railroad station in Obersdorf. We could store the items there indefinitely. This time no border guards were in sight when we crossed into Germany and went down the mountain to the ski lodge.

"You're back so soon," Mr. Meier said.

"We're anxious to get everything out," I told him. "We can't stay in Austria much longer. Our days are numbered."

Mr. Meier unlocked the door where we had placed our possessions. They were all there, just as he had said they would be. We thanked him for his help.

"Anytime," he told us, "as long as I have room."

We went on down to the bottom of the mountain and then several miles east to Obersdorf, arriving at the railroad station around noon. The clerk led us to some storage space. We put our things in the room, and the man gave me a ticket.

"You'll need the ticket when you come to get your stuff," he said. "That's the only way you can get it. They are very strict."

"I'll put it in a safe place," I assured him.

For the next several months the trips to Germany occupied my time. At least I had some goal to work toward, something to do. Maria and I made numerous trips to the ski lodge and the railroad station. Many times we saw the border guards. We lived with the fear of being detected and having our possessions confiscated, but we were willing to take the risks. One time Maria got a friend to take her to Germany in a car because she wanted to take some of our heavy silver across the border. At the checkpoint the guards confiscated the costly items. That experience convinced her that we should stick with the mountain. These trips were more strenuous but safer.

As the days passed, anti-German feelings became more and more apparent. The feelings had always been present, but the lax control observed by the French created a climate in which the resentment could be expressed openly. The Americans had held

a much tighter rein on the situation. Living in a deep
state of fear that something would happen to us, we
wondered how much longer we could last in such a
hostile environment.

One cold February day in 1946, a neighbor ran to
our door. I answered the knock.

"Has your mother seen the notice?" she asked me.

"What notice?" I asked.

"That we have to leave Austria."

"Mutti, come here," I called.

"What is it, Traugott?" She came down the stairs
from her bedroom to the front door.

"Hello, Mrs. Franz. Won't you come in?"

She stepped inside and shut the door.

"I can only stay a minute. I was just telling Traugott
about the notice."

"What notice is that?" Mutti asked.

"That we have to leave Austria. We must be in the
village in the morning. We can only take luggage,
nothing more."

"We knew that long ago," Mutti said. "Lucky we
planned ahead."

"I must go now and get ready," Mrs. Franz said. "I
hate to leave Austria, but I must stay with my husband. I never thought my own people would be so
cruel."

"War does terrible things," Mutti said. "Maybe one
day you both can come back."

"Maybe so."

Mrs. Franz excused herself and hurried home. Mutti turned to me. "Traugott, go read the notice yourself and make notes. Hurry!"

I ran to the village store where the notice was
posted. Everything Mrs. Franz had said was right. We
had to leave in the morning and go to the last place
we lived in Germany. For us, that was Augsburg.
Nine o'clock was the departure time.

That night we did most of our packing. Even
though we were glad to leave the Austrian hostility
behind, we felt a certain sadness and apprehension.

We didn't know what lay ahead. At one time we had had so much; now we would be homeless refugees. *This must all be a dream,* I thought. Life had been a nightmare for too long. How long could the nightmare last?

The Americans, the British, the Russians, the French, the two Austrians—they had caused all this. "I hate them all," I whispered before I fell asleep.

Early the next morning we walked to the meeting place. The trucks that were supposed to take us to Germany were parked along the main street. Mutti, Maria, and I got on the first truck.

Except for a very few kind people like Johann, we were leaving nothing behind. The bad experiences of the year overshadowed the good by a large measure. Even the pleasant childhood experiences at the lodge did not help. But time has changed things. Recently I went back to Austria with my wife and four children. The Austrians treated us royally. They want to forget how they treated the Germans. Every year many German marks are spent in the tourist trade there.

In the trucks we traveled from the French zone of Austria to the French zone of Germany. At Biberach we changed from trucks to the train. As we went down the street to the train station, I walked under a French flag. Suddenly a French soldier was standing beside me, glaring into my face. He grabbed my hat, threw it to the ground, and said something in French. I didn't know what he said, but I knew what his eyes said. For a minute I stared at him with a questioning look, glad that I couldn't understand his words. The hate in his eyes was more than I wanted to understand. I picked up my hat and walked on down the street.

We had a layover in Weingarten, so the three of us went to see Maria Eberhard, a lady who had painted our family portraits. I think she gave my mother some money while we were there. In later years, she told me how I impressed her at the time of our visit.

"When you came by," she told me, "you were very restless. You wiggled your jackboots so much that the sofa cover was black when you left."

She was right. I was restless—like a bomb ready to explode. Life was aimless and depressing. At that time, if anyone had asked me what I was going to do with my life, I would have been unable to answer. I had no goals. My goals began to fade with the death of my father and Germany's defeat.

After the short visit with Maria Eberhard, we continued on our journey, traveling north. All along the way we saw the rubble from the bombings and fighting. I saw Augsburg over and over again, with the Allied bombers.

Near Ulm the French turned us over to the Americans. As we went on through Ulm, I was confronted with an amazing sight. At the end of the street we were traveling on I saw the high steeple of the Lutheran cathedral. The entire building stood majestically in the midst of the ruins. It was not damaged. The sight was really impressive.

"Look," I said, pointing to the cathedral. Mutti and Maria looked up the street in that direction.

"Yes," Mutti said with little enthusiasm. They were not overly impressed. The rubble was too overwhelming, I suppose.

Five days after we left Reutte we arrived in Augsburg, with no idea of where we would live. Our house still stood, but someone else occupied the part that remained. We had no rights to the structure, anyway; ownership meant nothing. Like every other family that came to Augsburg, we went to the housing office to be assigned a place to live. They gave us a flat with two rooms and a tiny bathroom. Our quarters were so crowded that Mutti and Maria sometimes asked me to leave the apartment so that they could get dressed. Our income consisted of a widow's pension Mutti received from the state.

I roamed the streets and often joined in a soccer game. In the fall I reentered school and met old friends, some of them sons of Nazi officials. Things were not the same as before, though. The year lost in school was an embarrassment because some students thought I had failed. And the adjustment to the routine of school was extremely difficult. I felt that I had been required to be an adult so much that I couldn't be a child again. I had been out of school too long.

My SS background added to my already difficult adjustment. It was a heavy burden to bear, and there were always students ready to add to my burden.

"Traugott," a fellow student taunted me one day, "did you hear that the SS are criminals?"

I didn't reply. I had already heard about their status, and he knew it. That news had been very painful because I couldn't believe that my father would ever be considered a criminal. He was a patriotic man, and he was good.

For Germans, it was a time of trying to erase the past. Everybody wanted to escape the stigma of the Nazi regime. Anyone who had been connected with the Nazis could not teach or hold any significant position. To erase the past, adults went through a process of de-Nazification. People lied about each other just to escape the stigma. "He was worse than me" was a standard accusation.

But I couldn't escape from my past. When I could stand the pressure no longer, I quit school and walked the streets, looking for a job. Many times I stayed out most of the night, wandering aimlessly or sitting in the park. The apartment was so small, and money was scarce. I felt bad because I was not contributing anything to the support of the family.

After weeks of searching, I found a job in a library. There I met Berbel. She was pretty and full of life. For the first time in years, I looked forward to the next day and the next and the next. Still, it took very little to burst my balloon. The least little setback caused me to think, *If they hadn't killed my father, things wouldn't be so bad.* Hate for everyone who had caused my troubles was always ready to surface. It didn't take much to bring forth violent outbursts about the Americans, the British, the French, the Russians, or the Austrians—especially the two who killed my father.

7
Breaking the Vicious Circle

"A few days ago," a friend wrote to my mother, "I heard that some space is available in your mother's house. Why don't you come to Frankfurt?"

Mutti greeted me with the news when I came home from work. "Traugott," she said with unusual excitement in her voice, "we can live in Grandmother Ratazzi's home in Frankfurt."

"Oh, good," I said, trying to be enthusiastic. My impressions of Grandmother's home were not good. She was always so particular.

Maria was excited about the possibility of moving to Frankfurt and being able to live in a family home. But she wanted to stay behind in Augsburg to finish the school year. That was fine with Mutti. We had some friends she could live with.

The home in Frankfurt was the one my grandmother had bought shortly after Granddaddy's death. She lived there until she died in 1945. At that time no one looked for a relative to take over ownership. Instead, the state moved in several families whose homes had been destroyed by the bombs.

I was not the least bit excited about the move; moving meant that I had to leave my job at the library and my girlfriend. And Frankfurt was a new world, for we knew very few people there.

When we arrived in Frankfurt, we checked in at the housing office and got clearance to live in Grandmother's house. "The space in the attic is available," the clerk told us. We thanked him for his help and took the streetcar to the house.

"Living in the attic won't be much fun," Mutti said, "but maybe it won't be that way too long. Things are changing."

"It looks the same," I said when we got off the street-car in front of the house.

"Somehow it escaped with very little damage," Mutti said. "That's wonderful; otherwise the attic would be gone, and there would be no place for us to stay."

Since the front door was open, we walked on in. Mutti looked around at the furniture.

"The big clock is gone," she said, "and that inlaid desk, too. They have helped themselves to so much."

Many costly items were missing. And by the time all the families were gone, there was little left. But at least we were able to reclaim the house when many years later the families moved on.

We walked on up the stairs to our space in the attic, which consisted of a small dining room, bedroom, kitchen, and a tiny bathroom. These rooms had once been used for the maids' quarters and for storage. The space was limited, but it was an improvement over the apartment in Augsburg.

In Frankfurt I began to feel more independent than ever. At sixteen I was convinced that I should be my own boss. So when I wanted to go somewhere and Mutti said, "You better not go there now," I would ignore her and go anyway. Maria went her own way, too. In later years Mutti told friends, "My children never gave me any trouble." She just didn't remember.

Soon after our arrival in Frankfurt I began looking for a job, but there weren't many available for a teenager. Luckily, the owner of the electric company lived in our neighborhood; and he gave me a job as an office helper. It didn't take long to become dissatisfied with that job, though. "There's no future to it," I told Mutti. We discussed other possibilities. One possibility that appealed to me was undertaking a three-year apprenticeship as an office clerk. As I considered alternatives, I started leaning toward that type of program.

I went to several firms and applied for an apprenticeship. At each firm I presented a résumé of my education and family background. Always I included the fact that my father was an SS major; I had no choice. My past didn't help me one bit. Over and over, the people gave the same answer when I checked on my application: "I'm sorry, we have nothing available right now."

The explanations as to why nothing was available were vague. And no one encouraged me to check back later. No one ever admitted that my SS connection was a problem, but I knew it was. I knew of others who had applied for apprenticeships after me and who had been accepted already. Each time I told my mother about someone getting an apprenticeship when the person had applied after me, she ignored the problem.

"Maybe something will work out for you soon," she would say.

"You know it won't, Mutti," I told her after several discouragements. "They hold the past against me. It isn't fair."

"Just be patient," she said, "and keep trying."

All doors were closed. I didn't blame my troubles on my father, though; I blamed the people who were so prejudiced. They had no right to make me suffer for my father's patriotism. I kept looking and telling friends about my search.

"Maybe you can get a job with the Americans," a friend suggested.

The idea was repulsive. "Work for the enemy!" I snarled.

"The war's over," he said. "Besides, the pay is good. Do you know where the compound is?"

I told him I did, but we didn't pursue the subject

any further. For the time being, I dismissed the possibility of working for the Americans. I kept going to
the German businesses and kept getting the same
answer: "Sorry, we have nothing available." And I
kept hearing about people who got apprenticeships
at the same companies where I had applied.

After months of checking with the German firms,
I accepted the verdict and turned to the Americans.
In desperation and with great reservation, I went to
the employment office of the American military.

"What type of work do you want?" the receptionist
inquired.

"Any kind," I said. "But I prefer some kind of office
work."

"Do you have any experience?"

"Not really, just as an office helper."

She handed me an application. "Fill this out and
go to the second office on the right."

I filled out the application, went to the office, and
handed my application to the man sitting behind the
desk.

He glanced over the application and then told me,
"This isn't my area. Let me take you down the hall."

He took me to another office. I stood in the doorway
as he showed the application to the officer. The officer
frowned as he scanned the application. I got a funny
feeling in my stomach.

"Aaron would handle this," he said.

"All right, fine. I'll show him where to go." He sent
me to an office a few doors down the hall. "Room
110," he said.

A receptionist was assigned to the offices in that
area. "I need to talk with the officer in 110," I told her.

"OK," she said. "Just sit down and I'll tell Mr.
S........ that you are here." I couldn't understand the
name.

In a minute someone called my name. "Mr. Vogel,
won't you come in," the man said as he stood in the
doorway to his office. I stood up and walked the short
distance to the office.

"Sit down," he said, motioning to a chair.

"Thank you," I said and sat down in the chair in front of his desk.

"What do you want?" the officer said casually.

"I want work," I replied.

He shuffled through my papers, scanning the contents. He paused for a moment in one place. I tried to see where he was.

He must be reading about my dad, I thought, but I couldn't tell for sure where he was.

"How do you happen to know English?" he asked.

I felt a sense of relief. "I learned some in school," I told him. "And my mother taught me a good deal at home. She was born in Australia."

"I see . . . . That's an asset."

He looked down at the papers again. I watched him as he continued to read. He looked like my idea of the typical American—chewing gum and smoking at the same time.

At one point the officer shook his head back and forth and put his left hand to his forehead. My hands got clammy. "It's happening again," I thought. "I'm not going to get the job because of the SS."

The officer lifted his head up and looked me straight in the eye.

"If I treat you . . ."

Here it comes, I thought.

"Like your father may have treated my people . . ."

I broke the eye contact and looked at his hair and nose. *He's a Jew!* I gasped to myself. *What chance do I have now?* I had been taught what Jews were supposed to look like, and I now realized that he fit the description quite well. It seemed strange that I had not noticed before. But who would expect to see a Jew in the American military?

"It will be a vicious circle," he continued. My head reeled. I wanted to leave.

"Somewhere we must break the circle," he said firmly.

I looked straight into his eyes again. The words sounded hopeful.

"We'll give you a job and try you out," he told me. "If you do all right, you can keep the job."

"Thank you . . . thank you, sir." I was overcome with joy. Finally I had found an honest man. He had faced up to his feelings long before this meeting. Aaron was a German Jew who had immigrated to the United States and joined the army.

Aaron assigned me to the office of an engineering unit which was the central office for confiscated materials. My boss, Thomas T. Jackson, was a warrant officer from Pennsylvania. He was a great guy. He, along with some of the other workers in the office, gave me a nickname right away. "Traugott is too hard to say," they told me. "We'll call you Birdy." This was a translation of Vogel, which means bird. I did not object. In fact, I became attached to the nickname.

Jackson had a lot of confidence in me, and he opened up some opportunities that I had not expected to be a part of my job. On numerous occasions he asked me to interpret for the Americans when we went to warehouses where Germans worked. I really liked my job, and Jackson had a lot to do with helping me like it.

Jackson tried to loosen me up because he thought I was too solemn. "Birdy," he would say, "don't be so serious. You're going to be old before your time."

I interpreted his advice to mean that I should "live it up." So I began to smoke heavily and drink a lot. Occasionally I stayed out most of the night partying. I desperately wanted to be a part of the "in" group. I tried everything to be accepted, but there always seemed to be a closed door before me that I could not enter. I could join in a group but never feel a part of it.

A friend encouraged me to join a world citizenship organization. The idea appealed to me because I thought the organization would help me become part of the scene. Every day I was confronted with the reality of relating to many nations. At meetings of this organization speakers talked about all the people of the world getting together. That sounded good to me. My mother's background and attitude contributed to this feeling. She had gotten her Australian citizenship back and was bringing out her Australian connections more and more.

Most of all I wanted to learn everything I could about the Americans. I wanted to know what made them tick. Gradually I was overcoming my prejudice against the "bombers." But I was not yet committed to the idea of accepting them in a big way. At times they were still the enemy.

In the office I developed a good relationship with the other workers. I joked a lot with the American soldiers. I liked to jab them about their confined status. "Five o'clock comes, and I can go home," I would say. "I'm a civilian. I can go anytime I want. You have to get permission."

The Americans and I shared ideas, too. Often we did not agree, especially where democracy was concerned. This type of government seemed like an unworkable theory to me. The dialogues, though, were friendly for the most part.

On my birthday I arrived at work at the usual time. Although I was not late, I noticed that I was just about the last person to arrive.

"Well, well, look at all the early birds," I said.

They all laughed. "Always a first time for everything," one said.

"Even Walter's here on time," I said jokingly. "This has got to be the first time."

I hung my coat up and walked to my desk. Everyone followed.

"What's happening?" I asked.

"Nothing," Tom said with a smirk on his face. "We're going to get a drink of water."

"What is this!" I exclaimed.

Before me was a desk piled high with gifts. I

couldn't believe what was happening. By the time I got to my desk, everyone had gathered around. Their faces reflected my joy.

"How nice," I said, looking around at the group. "You shouldn't have done this. Thank you. Thank you."

One by one I opened the gifts and thanked the appropriate person. Inside I was overcome with surprise and gratefulness. I had forgotten that it was my birthday. But even if I had remembered, I would not have expected anything like a desk piled high with gifts.

Finally I came to the bottom of the stack. "This one looks interesting," I said. It was a long flat package. I read the tag out loud.

"To Birdy, from all of us."

"Hurry, open it," someone said.

As I tore the wrapping paper, I first saw a pair of slacks. Next I saw the jacket. The style definitely was not German.

"Why, it's an American suit!" I exclaimed. "How did you guess?"

I had wanted an American suit, but I couldn't buy one because Germans were not allowed to shop in the commissary. And I certainly would not have asked an American to buy it for me. That would have been going too far in accepting Americans—farther than I was ready to go at that time.

To top off the celebration, they sang "Happy Birthday." At the morning break we ate the birthday cake.

The American suit, along with an old officer's coat given to me by Jackson, became my passport to learn more about the Americans. These clothes opened the door to the officers' clubs.

I started with the NCO club. I wanted to know what happened inside. With German clothes on, I would never have been able to get through the front door. With the American suit, there was a possibility.

I told no one about my plans to go to the club be-

cause I decided to do it completely on my own. That
way no one else would be involved, and I wouldn't
have to worry about anyone reporting me to the
authorities. Friday night seemed like a good time to
make my debut. I smiled and said, "Hi," as I
walked through the front door. No one asked me for
an ID card or even questioned me. In my new suit
I looked like an American. But I knew if I said more
than "hi" I would be discovered.

I walked to a side area and surveyed the scene.
Some people sat at the tables, talking, eating, and
drinking. Others were dancing. The whole scene fascinated me. Since I did not have American money, I
didn't buy anything. And to avoid being detected,
I didn't sit with anyone. I just watched—and learned
about the ways of the Americans.

As I continued to observe the Americans, two men
walked in. They were military police—making their
rounds, I assumed. They glanced around the large
room. One turned to the other and said something.
The partner nodded his head in agreement, and the
two of them started in my direction.

What will I do? I thought. *If they catch me, I'll
lose my job.*

I looked for a place to hide; the two men kept coming toward me. Suddenly I saw the sign "Rest Rooms."
I darted toward the sign and followed the arrow to
the men's room. I ducked inside just as the police
walked by. When I thought they had left, I came
back out to watch the Americans.

My visits to the officers' clubs became a regular part
of my social life. On each visit I spent some time in
the rest room dodging the police. But it was all worth
the trouble. I enjoyed watching the Americans.

Things were not all pleasant, though. And the few
unpleasant experiences always revived past hatred
for the Americans. One day I overheard a sergeant
say to a lieutenant, "You can really scare these Germans." The sergeant was a bully.

I knew Henry, the sergeant, didn't like those "Krauts" even before I overheard his remark. He had guarded German POWs in the United States during the war. Now he couldn't seem to understand that the war was over, and he had no right to continue bossing the "Krauts." Often he came into the office screaming orders at the German girls.

I tried to ignore Henry, but the tension built. His condescending remark made me resent him more than ever. He had no idea that I had overheard what he said. *I'll show him,* I resolved, and I waited patiently for an opportunity to put him in his place. In my mind I rehearsed what I would say to him in certain situations and in response to particular remarks.

A few days later I got my chance. In his usual bully manner, Henry came into the office shouting and ordering the girls around.

"OK, everybody, get to work!" he yelled. "Coffee time is over. We have lots of work to do."

"Who's talking!" I snarled as he passed by my desk.

He reeled around and stared at me, obviously surprised and upset. I stood up and pushed my chair back. He was speechless. He didn't know how to respond to a challenge.

"We Germans," I began with emotion evident in my voice, "say 'Good morning' when we come into an office."

Henry looked startled, finding it hard to believe a German would have the nerve to stand up to him. I continued my speech while my co-workers looked on.

"We don't talk like this here in our country. If you want to learn some manners, go out with a German girl; and she will teach you what to say."

Henry regained his composure. "You better work," he threatened, trying to ignore my speech.

I turned around, sat down at my desk, and reached into the drawer. I put some gum into my mouth, lit up a cigarette, and propped my feet on top of the desk.

Out of the corner of my eye I saw the look of rage and utter frustration on his face. I put the cigarette in my mouth, inhaled deeply, and blew the smoke out my nose and mouth.

Henry stormed out of the office. Laughter erupted after he closed the door.

"I've been hoping someone would stand up to him like that, but I didn't have the nerve," one German girl told me. "Good going, Birdy."

"He's a big bully," another said. "I'm glad you put him in his place." Others expressed similar approval.

At closing time Henry came back into the office and walked straight to my desk.

"I want to talk to you, you German," he demanded.

"All right," I replied, "anytime."

"Right now!" he announced.

Henry sat down at the desk next to mine while everyone cleared out of the office quickly. When the last person went through the door, he stood to face me.

"So you're so big," he said, gritting his teeth. "Who do you think you are, you German?"

"I think I'm a human being," I replied.

He looked disgusted. "Ha!"

"Where is the democracy you brag about, anyway?" I demanded.

"Shut up, you German. You couldn't understand democracy. You don't know what it is."

"I know you're trying to treat us like prisoners. We're not supposed to be treated like that. The war is over."

"Shut up, you German. You're supposed to work."

"You're not my boss. The warrant officer is my boss."

"You're supposed to respect an American soldier."

"Officer Jackson is satisfied with my work. I don't have to answer to you."

Our voices were getting louder and louder. We were both practically out of our minds with rage.

"Shut up, you German," Henry yelled again. "You're supposed to respect an American soldier."

"It's stupid to scare people just for fun," I yelled back. "You're a bully."

"Shut up, you German," he shouted. "Shut up."

I couldn't stand the pressure any longer. I couldn't take one more "Shut up, you German." I lifted my arm, doubled my fist, and aimed for his mouth. I got a good hit. Then he hit back, and we exchanged several blows before we fell to the floor.

"You big bully," I said. "Picking on girls!"

"Shut up, you German."

We rolled over and over, trying to hit each other. I turned him over on his back and pinned him to the floor. He pushed me back.

Suddenly I saw someone standing beside us. As we rolled over, we both recognized Major Wilson. He had heard the noise and come from his office nearby to see what was happening.

"Men, what are you doing?" he said calmly.

We released our hold on each other and jumped to our feet.

"That German!" Henry exclaimed, pointing an accusing finger at me.

"That American!" I countered.

"He has no respect for an officer," Henry charged.

"That's not true. He's lying," I insisted.

I was too mad to pursue the matter anymore. I marched to my desk, and, with one stroke, cleared the top. Papers flew everywhere.

"I'm leaving," I blurted out. "I've had enough of this sort of guy." Henry's type was a minority; but at that moment, he was a majority—as far as I was concerned.

In a fast walk, I went out of the office and started down the long hall to the outside entrance. Major Wilson was close behind. He stood at the office door and called to me.

"Vogel," he said calmly, "you better be back here tomorrow morning. There's lots of work that needs to be done."

I heard his words clearly, but I did not stop to respond. I walked on out to the compound gate, anxious to get away from the Americans and reenter German society and the security of my home. At least I was accepted there.

The guard at the gate asked me for my pass. After I showed him the pass, I paused to look up at the tall barbed-wire fence that sealed off the compound from the outside world. *I wish those barbed wires were down,* I mused. The fence was a symbol of bigger barriers—barriers that I felt keenly in my state of intense anger and frustration.

As I stepped outside the gate, a sergeant approached me. He had a small stack of papers in his hand. "Have this," he said as he took a paper from the stack and held it out to me.

"What is it?" I snapped. I was in no mood to receive anything from an American.

"It's an invitation to a youth rally," he explained.

"What kind of youth rally?"

"A Christian youth rally."

I really laughed. "You're kidding," I said. This was the final insult to everything that had happened to me that day.

"No," I added with disdain. "That's not for me."

"Please . . . take the invitation," he urged, placing it in my hand.

"Are you a sissy," I sneered, using American slang.

He did not betray any dismay at my reaction. He simply listened and responded calmly.

"That's something for old people," I continued. "Old people go to church. Young people have more interesting things to do."

"Do come," he urged. "There will be many young people there."

I shook my head in disbelief, stuck the invitation in my pocket, and went on my way. Why I even kept the invitation, I don't know. I had no intention of going.

As I lay in bed that night I reviewed the experiences of the day. I concentrated on Major Wilson and what he had done. He was a kind man, I knew.

His facial twitches were evidence that he had suffered a lot himself. And sometimes his eyes did not focus exactly right. The war had taken its toll on him, but he was able to reach out to me.

Somebody cares, after all, I thought. I didn't have a father. That afternoon Major Wilson had been a father to me; he had given me some direction in life. In the darkness and quiet of my bedroom, I decided to go back to work the next day.

8
Who Lives?

After the war was over, it was not popular to be *Gottglaubig*. So my mother took her Protestant marriage certificate to the state office and applied for readmission to the Lutheran church. It was the thing to do. At the same time, she signed for Maria and me. Officially we were Protestants again, members of the state church. But we never went to church; we did not even have to go to church to join. Paperwork fulfilled the requirements for membership.

Actually, the only reason I had ever been inside a church was for culture, somewhat like visiting a museum. There were many beautiful churches in Germany. I had gone to see them on occasion to observe the architecture and to learn how the churches were a part of the history of Germany. Worshiping in a church was something I knew nothing about. And it was something that held no appeal for me.

Since I had completely dismissed the sergeant's invitation from my mind, I did not even feel that there was any decision to make. I had already made plans for Saturday night, plans I didn't want to change. I had a date with Iris, a girl I had met recently at a party.

Friday afternoon Iris called me at work.

"Birdy, line 1," Anna called to me. She had a silly smirk on her face. It was unusual for a girl to call me at work.

"Thank you," I said and picked up the phone.

"Hello. Vogel speaking."

"Traugott, this is Iris."

"Hi, how are things?"

"Well, I have complications tomorrow night. I'm afraid I'll have to break our date. My aunt is coming to see us, and I haven't seen her in a long time. I'm sorry."

"All right, Iris. I guess it can't be helped," I said, a little perturbed.

The excuse was so flimsy. I had a feeling that she was not telling the truth. *She surely knew about the visit,* I thought, *at least more than a day ahead.* But I did not argue.

"I'll see you later. All right?" she went on.

"Sure," I replied with little enthusiasm.

I sat down at my desk and worked quietly. No one probed about the phone call, and I offered no information. It was difficult to keep my mind on my work, though. A broken date was quite an insult, especially when the competition was an aunt.

All the way home from work I thought about what Iris had done. And the more I thought about her the madder I got. She had ruined my Saturday night. She had no right to do that.

"I'm going to confront her and find out why she broke the date," I decided.

Saturday morning I caught the streetcar near my home and went downtown. There I secured another ticket and boarded the streetcar that went to Iris's home on the other side of the city. *She's got her nerve spoiling my fun,* I thought as I rode along. I felt that it was too late to make other plans. An evening at home on Saturday night was not my idea of fun.

About halfway to Iris's house I reached into my coat pocket for my ticket. I knew the man would be collecting the tickets soon. First I pulled out a small piece of paper. It was blank on the side turned to me.

What's this? I said to myself. I turned it over to see what was on the other side. I recognized the invitation that the sergeant had given to me. I read it completely for the first time.

YOUTH RALLY
Christ's Chapel, Frankfurt Military Compound
Saturday Evening, February 21, 1948
Seven-thirty
Sponsored by the Frankfurt Youth for Christ
Everyone Welcome

I looked up from the invitation and considered the mission I was on. *What's the use of going to see Iris?* I thought. *She's not worth the trouble. Maybe I should go to a movie.*

I read the invitation again. My curiosity about Americans came to the forefront. Suddenly a thought came to me: *Well, I've seen what the Americans do in the officers' clubs, and I've seen them at work. Now I'd like to see what they do in church.*

At the next stop, I got off the streetcar and boarded a car going back downtown. Going to see Iris had been a silly idea, I decided. I didn't really know what I would have said to her anyway.

I arrived back home in the early afternoon. The explanation "I just went downtown to look around" was sufficient. No one asked for any additional information, and I was relieved.

At the evening meal my mother asked, "Are you going to a movie tonight, Traugott?"

"I don't know. I haven't really thought about what I'll do."

"There's a good movie at the Rex."

"Maybe I'll go look at the advertisements and then decide about seeing it."

I had already decided what I would do that evening; but to avoid any explanations, I didn't tell Mutti and Maria. And I really didn't know why I was going, anyway, other than curiosity.

I caught the six-thirty streetcar and went downtown. I got off the car in the center of the downtown area and walked a couple of blocks to catch the roundup car. This streetcar went to the area of Frankfurt where the American military compound was located. I knew the route well because I traveled it five days a week.

I got off in the center of the compound and walked the short distance to the gate, buttoning my coat to protect me from the cold winter wind. At the entrance I showed my pass to the soldier on duty and told him that I was going to the youth rally in the chapel. He looked a little surprised but said nothing. I did not have on my American suit, so he immediately recognized that I was German. Without further explanation, he let me go in.

Slowly I walked toward the wooden chapel, which was located at the north end of the compound. I walked past the building where I worked during the week. The Thursday experience with Henry came to mind. I cringed a little.

The chapel was an unpretentious building that was used by all denominations for church services. Originally the building had been called "Roundup Chapel" after the streetcar that went through the compound. Later it was renamed "Christ's Chapel."

Two men in uniform stood at the entrance to the chapel. Their greeting to me was unusually friendly.

"Welcome to the rally," one said with a big smile. "We're glad you've come." He handed me a program.

The other soldier led me to a seat in the auditorium and handed me a songbook. "Here's a good place to sit," he said. "Glad to have you."

I sat there quietly, surveying the crowd. The chapel was jammed. To my surprise, there were many young people in the crowd, most of them soldiers. Most of the people were Americans, with a few German visitors mixed in. The large gathering was impressive.

Why are so many people in a place like this? I

questioned silently. *Maybe they don't have anything else to do, either.*

The organ music began. I glanced in the direction of the music and noticed that a young man sat at the keys. Another young man sat at the piano, ready to begin.

Three men walked up the stairs to the platform. Two were in uniform; one was a civilian. One of the soldiers stepped up to the podium. He had a songbook in his hand.

"I want to welcome all of you to our rally tonight," he began. "If you have been here before, I say welcome back. If this is your first time to attend one of our Youth for Christ rallies, I want to invite you to come again. We're going to have a great time here this evening."

He displayed the songbook to the crowd. "I trust that all of you have found a songbook. Share your book with the person sitting next to you if he does not have one."

The song leader was bubbling with enthusiasm. I could tell everyone was ready to sing, including me, even though I knew none of the songs.

"Now will you join me," the song leader said, "as we sing 'He Lives.' You will find it on page 89 in your songbook." He lifted his hands and requested, "Let's all stand for this first hymn."

The crowd stood. The organ and piano sounded the introduction, and the crowd began to sing. As I had expected, the song was completely new to me. There were words that I had never heard spoken in English, such as "salvation" and "Savior." I had no idea what they meant.

"He lives; he lives," the song went. I wondered who lived. The affirmation didn't make sense to me because I didn't know who lived. I made a feeble attempt to sing along with the crowd.

On the second stanza I stopped to listen. The singing was so loud and full of feeling. I was filled with amazement that anyone could be so enthusiastic about anything that pertained to God. And the fact that so many in the crowd were young added to my amazement.

The hymn singing was interspersed with brief announcements. The guest speaker for the next rally was announced, along with an introduction of the speaker for the evening. Various activities sponsored by the Youth for Christ organization were previewed briefly. Attendance at the regular Saturday night rallies was emphasized.

After the special music by the choir, a man in uniform walked up to the podium. He had been introduced earlier in the service, but I had not paid much attention to him then. I looked at the insignia that identified him as an officer. *Why would an officer be speaking in church?* I wondered. I had noticed his rank before, but it was not until he rose to speak that I fully realized that an officer was speaking in church. He seemed so out of place.

The speaker made some brief opening remarks and then asked everyone to turn in their Bibles to 2 Corinthians 5:17. He began to read the passage. "If any one is in Christ, he is a new creation" (RSV). He read through verse 21.

The soldier sitting next to me shared his Bible so that I could follow the reading. Beginning with verse 17, the speaker proceeded to explain the meaning of the passage. He spoke as one who knew what he was talking about and that what he was saying was important. His confidence was impressive.

He talked about an individual becoming a completely new creature in Christ.

A new creature, I argued silently. *How can anyone become a new creation? You're what you make of yourself.* My dad had been a self-made man, I knew. He had accomplished something in life because he worked hard and took advantage of opportunities. The possibility that someone could step into a per-

son's life and make a new creation out of him was
beyond me.

The speaker expanded on his basic statement.

"Faith in Christ makes a person adopt new and
better goals. He has a new outlook on life. Life takes
on new meaning. He has a higher goal in life than
simply satisfying his own ambitions and desires."

"New meaning? New meaning?" The words caught
my attention. Did I ever need new meaning for my
life! I was groping in the dark. The man was so
sure that Christ could make a difference in my life!
But it all seems so farfetched, I thought. *A new creation, new meaning—in the twinkling of an eye.* It
couldn't be that easy.

He used a neon sign to illustrate his point. "All of
you have seen the neon sign advertising soap on
the highway," he began.

I had seen that sign many times. Soap bubbles were
continually produced only to disappear as fast as they
appeared.

"Without Christ," he continued, "life is like those
soap bubbles. You grab for them and feel a little mois-
ture in your closed hand. Then when you open your
hand, the bubbles have disappeared. You have nothing. You think a job is the answer to your yearning,
only to find that you go back to your original state
when the new wears off. You may go from one
party to another in an attempt to find satisfaction,
but it is not there. You grab for soap bubbles, but
they disappear."

*I've tried many things like that to find meaning in
life,* I thought. *So many things have seemed to be the
answer, but the excitement always fades away.*

Quickly I reviewed everything that had happened
so far in the worship service—the enthusiastic singing
filled with emotion, the dramatic appeal of the speaker. *This must be the real American way of worshiping
God,* I decided. *It's all emotion—too emotional for
me.* A cold, detached feeling came over me. *Maybe*

this is just soap bubbles. Maybe this man is deluded himself.

The speaker called me back to his message with these thoughts: "Even if you have lost everything, if you come to Jesus you will have a new life. This new life will really be everything. It's something you can hang onto. It's not soap bubbles; it's real."

His words sounded good. I was searching for something real, something that would last, something that would give life meaning.

What if this man is right? I asked silently. *What if this man is right?* I felt a little nervous inside, but I didn't know why.

The organist began to play softly. "We invite you," the speaker said, "to accept the new life in Christ. Think about it for a minute, then respond to the appeal of Christ."

The song leader rose. "The hymn of appeal is number 150," he said. "Let's all join in as we sing." Everyone, including me, turned to the hymn "Just As I Am." The song was completely new to me. Again there were unfamiliar expressions. The term "Lamb of God" really threw me. I had no idea wht it meant. It seemed so strange to connect a lamb with religion.

I noticed that most of the people sang without the aid of the songbook. They had the words memorized, although they did open their books. Again the people sang with unusual enthusiasm and feeling.

After the first stanza, the speaker motioned to the song leader. The song leader gave the appropriate signal for us to stop singing. The organist continued to play softly while the speaker made an appeal.

"We invite you to come to Jesus right now in this service. We invite you to commit your life to the One who can give life meaning. Won't you come now?"

He seemed to be speaking directly to me. I felt uneasy.

We sang the second stanza. The "one dark blot" and the blood that "can cleanse each spot" meant nothing to me. I didn't know what those words referred to. They were foreign to my experience.

Without any further word from the speaker, we began to sing the third stanza.

> *Just as I am, tho' tossed about,*
> *With many a conflict, many a doubt . . .*

I felt a lump form in my throat. I understood these words. I read them again as the crowd continued to sing. "Tossed about with many a conflict, many a doubt." The nervous feeling inside me increased.

Those words describe me, I thought. *That's me. I have many conflicts, many doubts . . . .*

"Let's sing that stanza again," the song leader said.

I was so choked up that it was difficult for me to sing. I continued to concentrate on the words "with many a conflict, many a doubt." I knew the words were so true. Inside I was in turmoil. I had a job I enjoyed and friends I could trust. I had all the invitations to parties that I wanted. Financially, I was better off than I had been in a long time. The war was over. But life had no real meaning. I had not found what I was looking for.

A young man stepped into the side aisle from the pew in front of me. He walked to the front of the auditorium. The speaker met him and shook his hand. After the two talked for a minute, the young man sat down in the first row.

Another man went to the front, and another, and another. They all talked to the speaker and sat down in the front row.

I shut my songbook and placed it in the holder on the back of the pew in front of me. "Excuse me," I said to the couple sitting beside me. They smiled and stepped into the aisle to let me out. I stepped into the aisle and walked toward the front, choking back the tears. The speaker met me at the end of the aisle and extended his hand to me. Then he glanced at my clothes.

"Oh, you're German," he said with surprise evident in his voice.

"Oh . . . is this just for Americans?" I asked defensively. "Maybe . . ."

"No, of course not. It's for everybody," he assured me.

He talked to me for a minute about Jesus and what my decision meant, then he asked me to sit down. "Sit here, and we'll talk more later," he told me, motioning to the front row where the other young men were seated.

The front pew gradually became filled with young people who had made decisions to commit their lives to Christ. For some, like me, it was the initial decision to commit our lives to Christ. For others, it was a decision to rededicate their lives to him. The number who responded was beyond anything I could have imagined.

When the invitation time was over, several men directed us to counseling rooms which were located in the same building. The speaker put his arm on my shoulder and took me to a room. This warm gesture made me feel good.

"I was surprised that you knew English," he told me after we sat down in the counseling room. "I thought I would have to get an interpreter."

I smiled. I had wrongly interpreted his surprise as a rejection of Germans.

"How did you happen to learn English?" he asked.

"My mother is an Australian," I explained.

He asked me a few questions such as where I lived, where I worked, how I happened to come to the meeting. He told me that he was a chaplain and what the title meant.

"Oh, you're a preacher," I said.

"Yes, that's right. I'm stationed in this compound."

For some reason I had never seen a chaplain during

the time that I had been working for the Americans.

"Are you a member of the state church?" he asked.

"I suppose so," I replied. "But I've never been to church until this evening."

We talked about the meaning of my decision. He opened the Bible, turned to the book of John, and asked me to read some verses. Of course, they were all new to me. We read some verses from the book of Romans, too. He read some and I read some. After each set of verses, he explained what they meant.

The chaplain, in a very gentle manner, spoke of Jesus standing at my heart's door, waiting for me to invite him in. He told me that I needed to ask Jesus to forgive my sins. I didn't ask many questions because I didn't know what to ask. I did know that I already felt a great sense of relief. I felt a peace inside that I had never known before.

"Will you kneel with me and pray?" he asked.

"I've never prayed in my life," I told him. "I don't know how."

The only prayer I was acquainted with was the Lord's Prayer and that only by name. Although I had never been to a Lutheran worship service, I knew the Lord's Prayer was recited there. I had heard friends jokingly ask each other, "Have you prayed your Lord's Prayer?" I didn't know the words in that prayer, though.

"What do I say?" I asked.

"Just talk like you always talk," the chaplain suggested. "And remember that God is holy."

We kneeled together beside the chairs. The chaplain waited for me to speak. I remembered what he had said about Jesus waiting for me to invite him into my heart.

"Jesus," I said. "Come into my heart. I need you." The tears rolled down my cheeks. I really meant what I said.

"Forgive me," I continued. "Help me."

I felt a joy and peace that had been beyond my reach until that moment. The chaplain was right.

Jesus could give life meaning. He could create a new person.

When I had finished praying, the chaplain prayed for me. He asked God to be with me as I started out in my new life. He prayed that God would give me strength and determination to live for Jesus. His prayer was warm and sincere and uplifting.

After the period of prayer, the chaplain showed me some pamphlets. "Study these, and if you have any questions, come to me. I'll try to help you." He urged me to come back to the Youth for Christ rally the next Saturday. He also mentioned the regular Sunday services at the chapel.

We walked together to the auditorium. Many people were standing at the front talking. A number stopped their conversations to greet me.

"We're so happy about your decision," one said. "You'll never be sorry."

"We'll be praying for you," a lady assured me.

"Christ makes life worthwhile," a young man told me.

"You have everything now," another added.

From the side aisle, a tall black man walked up to me, clapping his hands and smiling.

"I'm so glad! I'm so glad!" he exclaimed, taking hold of my hands. Tears were forming in his eyes. I suppressed my own tears.

"I'm so glad you came to Jesus," he continued.

"Thank you," I mumbled. I was so overcome with emotion that I could hardly speak.

"When I saw you come into the worship service with your stern face, I knew you were not a Christian. I began to pray for you."

I looked at him in amazement. *Why would a black man pray for me?* I wondered. I had never met a black man like this before. The only image I had of black men was the one created for me during the war.

"Keep praying for me," I said.

"I will," he assured me.

"Thank you," I said and turned to leave.

"Come back next week," he called after me.

"I will."

I left the chapel with the deep assurance that I was headed in the right direction. I wanted to return for the next Saturday night rally. That Iris had broken a date with me was now a cause for rejoicing.

9
Where Are the Words?

It was a few degrees colder when the rally ended. I buttoned my coat all the way to the top, turned the collar up, and pulled my hat down over my ears. In a brisk pace I walked to the compound gate, showed my pass to the guard, and went across the street to wait for a streetcar. Within ten minutes one was there ready to board passengers.

When we arrived in the downtown area, it was still early—too early to go home on a Saturday night. For a couple of hours I walked around downtown, thinking about the meeting and the decision. The words of the preacher came to mind over and over— "If you have Christ, you have everything." The warm feeling within, along with the sense of relief and peace, made his statement ring true. But I wondered how I would explain my feelings to Mutti and Maria. They wouldn't understand. I slipped into the house without saying anything to either one of them.

"Did you find something interesting to do last night?" Mutti asked at our late breakfast the next morning.

"So-so," I replied.

"I thought you had a date," Maria chimed in.

"Naw. I just fooled around with the boys."

"But . . ." Maria insisted. "You did have a date, didn't you?"

"No, Maria. I didn't. Now will you forget it."

"Pardon me, Mr. Pleasantness!"

"Oh, I'm sorry. I didn't mean to be so grouchy."

Maria's mouth flew open, but she couldn't think of

anything to say. She wasn't accustomed to apologies. Mutti looked a little startled, too.

I wanted to tell them about my decision, but the words just wouldn't come out. I knew they would think it was all make-believe.

"I'm going downtown," I told Mutti when we finished eating.

"Again? What for?"

"Just to fool around. Albert and I might go to a movie."

"We're eating at six, so be back then if you plan to eat with us."

"All right. I'll probably be back, but eat without me if I don't make it."

I mentally kicked myself all the way downtown. *Why didn't you say anything?* I asked myself over and over. But what could I say? Everything was so new. How can a person explain an experience he hardly understands himself? One excuse after another came to mind, and they all sounded good.

I walked around downtown window-shopping and thinking—thinking about the music and the sermon, thinking about what the chaplain had told me after the service in the counseling room.

"The best thing you can do right now," he had said, "is tell someone about your experience here tonight. Sharing your experience with a friend will make it more real to you. And the more you relate the experience the better you will be able to explain what has happened within you. And the better you will understand it yourself."

I walked around until time for the Sunday matinee. A comedy was showing at the main theater. I chose that offering because something on the light side sounded good. When the movie was over, I found a restaurant nearby. Going home to eat didn't appeal to me. After the evening meal I found another movie— not very interesting, but something to do, anyway. When I got home, Mutti was going to bed, and

Maria was still out on a date. I breathed a sigh of relief and went to my room.

The next morning Mutti had breakfast ready at the usual time. I came down before Maria to greet her.

"Good morning, Mutti," I said as I walked into the kitchen.

"Good morning, Traugott. We missed you at supper last night."

"I just stayed downtown and took in a couple of movies."

"Oh. And you ate down there, too?"

"Yes. At the Italian restaurant."

"Did Albert go with you?"

"No, he had a date."

"You went alone?"

"Yes. All alone. But I didn't mind."

She looked surprised but pursued the subject no further.

"Did you stay home?" I asked.

"No. I visited next door until about ten-thirty. It was fun. They are very nice people."

"Yes, they seem to be nice. I . . ."

"Well, Traugott is here!" Maria exclaimed as she bounded into the room. "We haven't seen much of you this weekend. Where have you been?"

"Oh, here and there."

Soon Mutti had breakfast ready, and we began to eat. Maria and I talked about things that had happened at work the week before. Mutti talked about the British women's club she had joined, where she met a number of people of Australian and British background. We talked about everything—everything except the Youth for Christ meetings at the compound.

Monday was a rather routine day at work. Henry didn't even come around with his obnoxious shouts. At the morning coffee break, a few of us stood together talking about the activities of the weekend.

"I'll bet you hung one on this weekend, Birdy," Jack suggested, laughing.

"No, not this weekend," I replied, smiling.

"Then what did you do?"

"I went to the rally."

"What rally?"

"The rally in the chapel."

A faint smile came across his face. The others in the group stared at me in disbelief.

"You gotta be kidding. You went to that! How did you happen to go there?"

"The sergeant outside the gate gave me an invitation, so I went. I wanted to see how you Americans act in church."

"Ooooooh. Well, my Saturday night wasn't quite that tame," Ted said, laughing. "Madeline and I went to a big blast downtown."

Quickly the conversation went to descriptions of the Saturday night escapades. No one else mentioned the rally or wanted to know more about it.

In the afternoon a sergeant walked near my desk. He put his hand on the side of the desk and leaned over to me as if preparing to tell a joke or something in confidence.

"Hey, what's this I hear about you getting religious?" he asked. "Is that true?"

I felt a little uneasy, not knowing exactly what to say. But I had to respond. "I've given my life to Jesus, if that's what you mean."

"It's really true what they say then."

"I feel great!"

He shook his head in disbelief. "It won't last. I've seen others do the same thing. They're good for a while, and then. . . ."

"Well, maybe they weren't determined. I am."

"See ya around," he replied with a skeptical look on his face.

I thought the day would never end. This new relationship with the Americans was a drain emotionally. At this point I wasn't quite sure how to relate to them.

I knew that I was not the same Traugott Vogel, but did they? Since I was a German, my inclination was to approach the situation with extreme caution. I was the outsider.

It was a great relief when closing time came and I could leave work behind me. On the way to the streetcar I felt an arm on my shoulder.

"Hi, Traugott. How are you doing?"

"All right. After a hard day's work," I chuckled.

"You may not remember me. I'm Larry, from the Youth for Christ meeting."

"Oh, yes. It's good to see you."

"You've made a great decison."

"Yes, I'm sure of that, too."

"Are you coming Saturday night?"

"I plan to."

"See you then."

"Good."

Thank you, Lord, I sighed to myself as Larry went on his way. *I needed that word.*

Once downtown, I got off the streetcar and went to a bookstore to look at Bibles. The bookstore owner explained some of the special features of a German Bible I picked up.

"This Bible is a big seller," he told me. "It's not too big and not too small. And the concordance is especially helpful."

"Oh," I responded blankly. I had no idea what a concordance was, and he knew it. So the man turned to the back section of the Bible to show me.

"Look here," he said, "here's the word 'love.' If you want to read some on this subject, you just look up the Scriptures that are listed under that heading."

I bought the Bible, tucked the package under my arm, and walked around for a while, trying to decide what to say to Muttie about the decision. The pressure was mounting.

At supper there was no opportunity to say anything. After we ate I excused myself to read in my room. I got out the pamphlets the chaplain had asked me to study. One dealt with "understanding your decision." In my new Bible I read the Scripture passages listed under this topic. The first passage was in the third chapter of John's Gospel. It was Nicodemus' conversation with Jesus about being born again. I read John 3:16 again—"For God so loved . . . ." The words were thrilling. How could he—why did he so love? I wiped the tears from my eyes, but they were replaced by others. "Oh, God, thank you," I sobbed. For a few minutes I let my emotions go. The tears of joy flowed.

I read the pamphlets over and over again, along with the Scriptures suggested for additional study on each subject. One Scripture was Matthew 10:32— "Whosoever therefore shall confess me before men, him will I confess also before my Father which is in heaven" (KJV). Mutti needed to know about my decision. "Lord, give me the courage to tell her," I prayed out loud.

All the way home from work the next day I rehearsed a speech for Mutti. I had to tell her before someone else did. Nothing sounded good, though; it all came out too pious, too farfetched. Being saved, converted. What could that mean to my mother? *Why is it so hard to talk about an experience that means so much?* I asked myself once more. An answer to the question eluded me.

That evening the opportunity came. Maria had gone out on a date, and Mutti was reading in the living room. She looked up when I walked in. I picked up a magazine and began reading. My hands became clammy; a nervous feeling developed in my stomach. My throat felt dry. Several times I started to say something, but the words wouldn't come out. It was all so ridiculous. Finally I forced myself to speak.

"Mutti," I began softly and seriously.

"Yes," she said, looking up from her book.

"I have something I want to tell you."

"Oh, what is it?" She looked surprised and a little worried.

Everything was coming out so serious. The happiness, the enthusiasm, the great feeling inside were not in the forefront. For Mutti, this one who was so dear to me, it would not be joyful news—I was afraid. I wanted her to know that it was all wonderful, but the words just wouldn't come out that way. I tried to change the mood.

With a big smile I announced, "I gave my life to Jesus!"

There was a long moment of silence as she considered what I had said.

"Oh, when did this happen?" she asked, with a bewildered look on her face.

"Saturday night."

"Where?"

"At the youth rally at the military chapel."

"So that's where you were Saturday night."

"That's right."

"Why did you go there?"

"I just wanted to see what Americans did at church."

"And you liked what you saw?"

"Yes, but it's not only an American thing. It's for everybody."

"Oh," she responded, with skepticism in her voice.

"I've let Jesus come into my heart. I'm going to live for him."

"Are you religious now?"

"I'm a new person. Jesus has made me a new person."

"Oh . . . but the Americans have all emotion in their religion."

"It's hard to explain, and I know it's hard for you to understand, but I feel different about things now. And its not just emotion. It's in my head, too. I am going to live my life for Jesus."

She did not respond. It was evident that she did not understand what I was talking about. And maybe she thought the mood would pass. Her real questioning came a few years later when I was baptized. But no matter what I did or said, she never complete-

ly understood what happened to me that Saturday
night in February, 1948.

Circumstances of life had made me a lonely person. In Austria I had had few friends because of my
father's SS connections. This association had continued to be an obstacle after we were resettled in
Germany. Then, with the Americans, there were walls
set up because of cultural differences. And the mo-
bility of the Americans made it difficult to develop
close friendships. Only I was really aware of the
barriers, though. As far as other people were concerned, there was no big problem. Becoming a Christian did not solve all my problems. In fact, my new
status actually increased my loneliness because I had
to make a complete break with my past. None of my
former friends were committed to Christ. I had to
find a new circle of friends.

The Youth for Christ rallies became my main
source of Christian fellowship and friendship. In a
way, the Youth for Christ group became my whole
life. After the first rally, I returned the next Saturday
night and the next and the next. Eventually I became
a council member of the Frankfurt Youth for Christ.
In that capacity, I helped plan the rallies. And along
with the rallies, I regularly attended Sunday School
and church services at the military chapel in Holchst,
a short distance from Frankfurt.

Two people in the Youth for Christ helped me
greatly in my new life—Larry and Inge. Larry was
an American GI. He was a tall, rugged-looking fellow
who had grown up on a farm. During the winter
months he always wore a long American coat. He
seemed to have a lot of confidence in himself.

Often Larry and I rode on the streetcar together to
and from the Youth for Christ meetings. Always he
took advantage of opportunities to tell others about
Christ. I was impressed with the way he talked to
people.

"You're really doing a good job talking to the people," I told him.

"That's what we're supposed to do. We're supposed to witness."

When I had an opportunity I tried to follow Larry's example. And gradually I developed my own way of talking to people about Christ. When Larry was sent back to the United States, his going was a great disappointment. He was the closest friend I had made among the Americans.

Inge was my first Christian girlfriend. Being a German, she helped bridge the gap that was developing between me and my own people. At times I felt more like an American than a German.

Inge and I first met at a Youth for Christ rally. She was there with some German friends. We started meeting at the rallies every week, and I would take her home afterward. Gradually our relationship deepened.

One Saturday night Inge didn't show up for the rally. I went by her house to see what had happened.

"Inge is at her aunt's house," her mother told me. She didn't invite me in. Her manner was so distant. I wondered why.

In a couple of weeks Inge came to the rally.

"Why haven't you been here?" I asked. "I've missed you."

"I've missed you, too. My parents had things planned."

That wasn't the whole story, I knew. On the way home I pressed her further.

"What's the real reason?" I insisted.

"OK, I'll tell you. They just don't like for me to be around the military so much. You know what the Germans think about GIs."

"I'm not a GI, though."

"But you're around them so much. You're so much a part of them."

"The Youth for Christ is different."

"I know. But they don't know that."

"Still, try to come," I urged as we said good-night. "The rallies mean so much to me."

"I'll try."

"I love you," I told her as I held her in my arms and kissed her.

"I love you, too."

Inge and I kept meeting at the rallies and sometimes during the week. It always took a lot of persuasion for her parents to let her come to the rallies.

The same year that I was converted, I started a three-year apprenticeship to become an office clerk. The work with the Americans had opened the way to a job with my own people. I served my apprenticeship at a leather factory in Offenbach, the leather town of Germany. Early each morning, I cycled the few miles along the Main River to go to work.

One morning at coffee break I met a young man named Hans. I wanted him to know about the Youth for Christ rallies. I tried to be as relaxed as Larry when I approached him.

"Have you heard about the Saturday night rallies?" I asked.

"What rallies?"

The Youth for Christ rallies?"

"No, I've never been. Are you a Christian?"

"Yes. You, too?"

"Oh, yes, two years now. I go to a German church."

What a thrill to find someone who knew how I felt! For a few minutes we shared our conversion experiences. Unlike me, he was converted among the Germans, and worshiped with the Germans.

Hans talked to me about volunteer YMCA work among the Germans. He was heavily involved in the work. Working with young people in that particular type of work had great appeal for me, and I decided to join Hans. After a period of training, I was assigned to a troop of young German boys in Offenbach, where Hans also was a troop leader.

Along with Inge, the YMCA work occupied most of my spare time—going on outings, participating in training workshops, and guiding special projects. I also attended several regional conferences in Germany; and, because of the contacts made at these conferences, I was elected from the Protestant wing to be a member of one of the first youth city parliaments in Offenbach. These parliaments were organized because the Americans felt that young people should be taught democracy. On retreats we learned the basics of democracy and the basic laws of government. We studied the new German constitution in detail. For a year I participated in this training and gradually came to feel that democracy might be the best type of government.

A victory achieved by means of the democratic process was the final convincer. We had a large sum of money designated for youth work. The Catholic group wanted to use it for a carnival. The Protestant wing wanted to use the money for a youth project. And we began to campaign for our cause. We secured support from the other elements in the Parliament, including the Communists. The excitement was so widespread that we received press coverage. We won, and the money was used for a youth project. It was a big victory for the democratic process.

During the years of apprenticeship and working with the YMCA, I had kept in contact with the Youth for Christ organization. Inge and I went to the rallies together almost every Saturday night. One day I heard that some Youth for Christ leaders were in Frankfurt, attending a special conference in a hotel downtown. At the meeting Chaplain Paul Maddox introduced Dawson Trotman, founder of the Navigators, a group concerned with following up new Christians. Trotman's explanation of the Christian life was impressive. He pictured it as a wheel which had as its spokes the Word of God, prayer, witness, and life.

After the meeting, when the group was walking down the stairs, I felt a hand on my shoulder. I turned around.

"Who are you, and how do you happen to be here?"

the man asked. It was Dawson Trotman. Possibly he singled me out because I was about the youngest person at the meeting.

"I'm Traugott Vogel. I attend the rallies at the military compound." I went on to tell him that I had been saved at a Youth for Christ rally at the military chapel. I also told him something about my YMCA work.

Trotman communicated a feeling of love and concern for me. I was surprised that he was so interested in what I was doing. When we came to the main door of the hotel, we could see that it was raining outside. Trotman unfolded his raincoat and held it out to me.

"Here, take this," he said.

"But you need it," I replied.

"No, I want you to have it," he insisted. "And give me your address." He put the raincoat on my shoulders and pulled out a piece of paper and a pencil and wrote down my address.

Not long after the meeting, Trotman sent me a letter. This started a correspondence of encouragement that lasted a number of years. At Trotman's funeral, Billy Graham affirmed that this man must have touched more lives than any man he knew. I was one life that he touched.

My activities in the Youth for Christ movement broadened. I began to participate in open-air meetings and periodically went with a team to churches in other towns. On one occasion an American civilian Youth for Christ worker named Harold asked me to go with him to a Protestant church in a town near Frankfurt. He knew that I had interpreted a lot in connection with my job at the leather factory, and he wanted me to interpret for him as he preached. I had never interpreted for the gospel message, but I felt confident that I could. Because of past successes, I was sure I could do a good job.

We traveled by car to the church and arrived promptly at seven o'clock. The elders greeted us in front of the church and showed us where to go. We had time to get acquainted and join in a prayer time before the worship service.

On the platform I sat beside Harold, waiting to interpret for him. As usual, we sang a few songs and took an offering; then Harold rose to speak. I stood beside him, ready to translate his English into German.

"Turn with me to Hebrews 4," Harold asked the congregation. I stumbled over the words. Harold remained composed as I tried to form the very simple words he had spoken. Finally and slowly they came. All over the auditorium people opened their Bibles as I finished the sentence. I opened my German Bible to the passage.

Harold read Hebrews 4:14: "Seeing then that we have a great high priest, that is passed into the heavens, Jesus the Son of God, let us hold fast our profession" (KJV). I read the words from my German Bible enthusaistically and with great ease. Verse by verse we read alternately until we came to the end of the chapter. Then Harold began to explain what the passage meant.

"Jesus Christ is a priest who understands us," he said.

"Jesus Christus ist ein . . . uh . . . uh . . ." The word for "priest" eluded me. The entire congregation stared at me, waiting. Out of nowhere the word came. "Priester der . . ." The word for "understand" wouldn't come. Finally I did remember it and finished the sentence. But the pressure was building. My mouth felt dry, my hands clammy. *What is wrong?* I wondered.

"He knows how we feel because he has been where we are," Harold continued.

My mind was completely blank. "He knows; he knows," I whispered in English. I couldn't remember. I looked down at my feet. I looked at Harold. I looked at the people. They stared back at me, obviously embarrassed—for themselves and for me. I just couldn't remember the words—words of my native tongue. They were such simple words, and Harold spoke so clearly. It was unbelievable, incredible!

One of the elders raised his hand and motioned for me to come down from the platform. With everyone watching, I bowed my head and walked down the aisle to a rear seat. My face was burning. The man seated next to me gave me a quick glance and then abruptly turned to face the platform.

The elder sent a high-school boy to take my place on the platform beside Harold. I broke out in a hot sweat. What an insult! A schoolboy. I got up and left the auditorium. Without any plan, I turned south when I went out the front door. For ten or fifteen long minutes I walked down the street, wondering what had happened. An explanation was beyond my understanding; it all seemed like a bad dream, unreal.

The street came to a dead end, and I faced a tall fence. I couldn't go any farther. So I just stood there, hanging on to the fence, moving it back and forth.

Running away is no solution, I told myself, acutely aware that I was making the problem worse. I turned around and began walking in the direction of the church. *I have to face them,* I decided.

Harold was still preaching when I walked back into the church and sat down near the back of the auditorium. With my eyes wide open, I began to pray for the interpreter. That was something I had not even done for myself, because I had approached this assignment like any other interpreting assignment. But communicating and proclaiming the gospel is not like any other assignment. It is not like closing a deal between a leather factory and an important customer who speaks a different language. It is not like serving as an interpreter at leather trade fairs. *The gospel message is special,* I thought. *And what a painful way to discover that truth.*

To my surprise, the young interpreter got better and better as I prayed. He did not miss a word, and the words were filled with enthusiasm. He was not only translating; he was communicating.

None of the elders talked to me after the service, and a very few people expressed halfhearted pleasure that I had come to visit. Their actions added to my embarrassment. *Maybe they just don't know what to say, so they say nothing,* I reasoned, trying to excuse the elders. Still, it was a blow. And when Harold signaled that he was ready to go, I had a feeling of great relief.

"That was a tough break," Harold said when we got into the car. "You just froze, I guess, but it could happen to anybody."

"I'll never interpret again," I said.

"Oh, don't let that experience tonight discourage you. It could happen to the best. You're a good interpreter."

"I don't want to go through that again."

"But maybe that's just what God wants you to do," Harold suggested.

"I doubt that."

It wasn't long before Harold asked me to go with him again to interpret. His trust was encouraging. My approach was different this time. Prayer—real prayer —was a part of the preparation. And I was a participant rather than a bystander simply performing a job.

More and more invitations came to interpret. As I interpreted in the various meetings, God began to speak to me about preaching. For several weeks I thought about the possibility, not overly anxious to make a decision. The fact that my mother would be shocked by such news held me back. But at an open-air meeting at the Frankfurt Railroad Station the feelings became intense.

To the huge crowd in front of the station, our Youth for Christ team leader announced that copies of the Gospel of John were available for all who wanted them. The pamphlets were stacked on a table in front of the crowd, and anyone could pick some up after the meeting.

In the front row I saw three tough-looking men dressed in heavy padded black jackets. Those jackets identified them as POWs who had been held in Siberia during the war. The three men listened intently to the sermon; and after the meeting, they came and asked for copies of the Gospel.

Their interest was surprising and thrilling. I had to find out more about them. "Why would you be so interested in John's Gospel after being to hell and back?" I asked.

"That's where we began to search for God," one of the men replied. The other two nodded in agreement. "We got to know a man who told us about Christ, but we didn't take him seriously then."

As the three men walked away, I was really impressed with the idea that preaching the gospel was important and urgent. And I wanted to communicate the gospel in my own language rather than simply interpreting for another.

Just before going to sleep that night, I thought about the three men in the padded jackets, three tough men who had responded to the gospel. There were so many like them who needed to know that Christ could help them. They needed to know that Christ could help them overcome the past and point them in a new direction. Germany was filled with such people.

I threw back the covers, knelt beside my bed, and prayed. "If you want me to go preach the gospel, I will," I told God. As I surrendered my life completely to him for this purpose, I knew he was saying, "Yes, I do want you to preach the gospel. I've been waiting for your answer."

Never again did I see the three men in the black-padded jackets—the ones who had played such a dynamic role in my decision without knowing it.

10
Launching Out

In March of 1951 I received my apprenticeship diploma and decided to go back to work for the Americans. But the way events developed, I only worked in the compound for six months.

During the short period of reemployment with the Americans I met an Englishman named John Thomas at one of the Youth for Christ rallies. While we talked after one of the rallies, I shared with him my deep desire to train for my calling. He told me about the Bible College of Wales, an interdenominational school that had been very pro-Jewish during the war. Rees Howells, the founder of the school, had written a book before the US entered the war in which he predicted the downfall of the Nazis. And all during the war, the students at the college had prayed for the Jews in Germany.

Inge stood by my side as I talked to Thomas. She said nothing.

"Would you go clear across the ocean to go to school?" she asked on the way home.

"Yes, if I felt that was what the Lord wanted me to do."

She looked disturbed. "But England is so far. I'll never see you again."

"Yes you will. I'll get back. But I haven't left yet, anyway. That may not be what God has in mind."

"I hope it isn't." She looked so troubled.

"I do want to train for my calling," I told her.

"It's so far, though, so far."

Soon after talking with Thomas, I received a brochure that contained information about the college. After examining the brochure, I came to the firm conclusion that it was just the place for me to train.

When I showed the brochure to Mutti and Maria, their reaction was negative—as I had expected.

"You're really going off the deep end," Mutti chided. "What's wrong with you; why are you taking this religion business so seriously?"

"It's important to me, Mutti. I wish you knew how important it is."

"Why do you want to go out of Germany? There are good schools here."

"I just feel that Wales is the place for me to go."

"But Traugott, you don't make sense. How do you know they'll accept you, anyway?" Mutti continued.

"I don't know. I'll just have to apply and wait."

"This is so foolish," she sighed, clasping her hands tightly on her lap. "You have a good job with the Americans, and you're just going to throw it all away."

Maria said nothing, but I could tell she agreed.

A couple of weeks later I received the letter of acceptance and showed it to Mutti.

"See. I've been accepted," I said. "I knew they would let me come."

She looked blank as she read the letter and only asked, "What about a visa? That may be difficult to get."

"I'll get it," I replied confidently. "I'll get it. I know I will."

Securing a visa to Great Britain turned out to be a longer process than I had anticipated. It was not easy for a German to study abroad because we were still suspect. And my SS background continued to dog my steps. It added to the already difficult process. The only thing in my favor was my mother's Australian citizenship and the fact that she had a friend in the consulate whom she had met in her club.

A month passed and no answer came. In between each trip to the British consulate to check on the progress, there was complete silence. They said nothing one way or another. Each time I made an inquiry, the answer was always, "We're working on it. We'll let you know when they tell us."

Two months passed and still no visa. And as I waited the old resentment came to the forefront.

The Americans were no help either. They wanted me to stay at my job. "You've got a good future in this work," my boss told me. "You've made good progress, and you're making good money." There was a time when that would have sounded good, but time had changed things.

"This is something I must do," I insisted; but they, like Mutti and Maria, didn't understand.

Three months passed and still no answer. Doubts arose. *Is this really God's will?* I began to ask myself. *Why isn't it working out, if this is what he wants me to do?* The confidence that "I need to go" grew weaker and weaker. *I can witness on my job,* I thought, *and then work on special projects in my spare time. Maybe the obstacles are meant to point me in another direction.* I knew there was a chance that I had misinterpreted what God wanted me to do. I began to consider other possibilities.

Finally, after more than three months of waiting, word came. "You got a letter from the British consulate today," Mutti told me when I came home from work.

"Where is it?" I exclaimed.

"On the table," she replied with little enthusiasm.

I rushed to the dining room and tore open the letter. The message was brief. Mutti stood in the doorway as I read it.

"My visa has been approved!" I shouted. "I can't believe it."

Mutti looked stunned. "The one obstacle has been removed," she said with resignation.

"I guess the consul became convinced that I was sincere. And maybe your friend helped, Mutti."

"Maybe so, but I never asked for a favor. I was hoping you would come to your senses while you were waiting. But you're more determined than ever. It's all beyond me," she sighed.

"Oh, Mutti," I said, taking her in my arms. "I wish you could understand. Maybe you will someday. It's a great life!"

Oh, how I wished she understood and could share in my joy. I loved her so. She had always been so interested in everything I did, so concerned about what I did with my life. But this religion business was another matter.

"But why do you have to do it as a full-time thing?" she asked. "Why are you taking this religion so seriously?"

"You just don't understand. This is something I must do and want to do. It's exciting."

"You're going crazy. Just read your Bible and keep your job."

"That would be fine for many people. But not me. God has called me to preach, and I must prepare."

She shook her head in disbelief and despair. Some time later she told a friend, "If I had the means I would send Traugott to the university to study for the state church." She felt it was foolish to go out of the country to study at a small college that had no prestige as far as she was concerned. Who in Germany had ever heard of the Bible College in Wales?

The next day I told my boss the news. He congratulated me. Then a couple of days later, he called me into his office.

"Birdy," he began, "I know you've made a lot of plans already, but I received approval to talk to you about another job."

"But ..."

"Just let me tell you about the job first. All right?"

"All right."

"You know what Harry does, don't you?"

"Yes, of course. He has a good job."

"Well, he is going back to the States."

"Really?"

"Yes. Do you think you would enjoy his job?"

"Certainly. He has a lot of responsibility. But I've made plans."

"And the pay increase would be considerable," he went on, ignoring my last statement.

"It is tempting, but . . ."

He interrupted me to continue telling me about the job, emphasizing the good points. "Now, you don't have to give me an answer right now. But I do want you to think about it. Just let me know in a couple of days."

"All right. I'll do that," I said as I got up to leave.

The offer was more tempting than I had realized it would be. That night I didn't sleep much. I kept thinking about the job. *I would be near Inge,* I thought.

I wrestled with the decision all night. In the morning I had come to a decision. I had to turn the job down.

"I'm sorry to hear this," my boss told me when I gave him my answer. "You may be sorry."

"Maybe. But I don't think so."

He wished me well in my new venture, but I could tell he questioned my judgment.

Except for my Youth for Christ friends, there were few who encouraged me. My mother and sister thought I was going off the deep end. My co-workers thought I was crazy to turn down a good job. And Inge wasn't happy about the developments either.

"I'll never see you again," she sobbed one evening as we walked around downtown.

"But you will," I assured her once again. "And we can write to each other."

"Why can't you stay in Germany? There are good schools here. Why don't you stay with your own people?"

"I just must go, Inge. I wish you could understand."

"I don't," she replied firmly.

Shortly before the time to leave, Inge and I broke up. This parting was painful, but it was another

thing that made it easier for me to follow through on
the decision to go to Wales. More and more I became convinced that I was following the right course.

As the departure time arrived, finances became a
factor. I had saved some money for my first year at
Wales, but I also was depending on the last paycheck
for my work with the American military. I waited
for a couple of weeks, but the check did not come.
Finally I went to the payroll officer.

"Do you need it right now?" the man asked.

"Yes, I do," I told him. "I'm scheduled to leave the
country in a few days."

"What type of work are you going to do?"

"I'm going to Bible college."

"Oh. Where?"

"In Wales. And I'm going to trust in God, just like
it says on your money."

He looked a little surprised. "That's a good comparison. Just wait a minute, and we'll have things
worked out."

A few minutes later he came back to the front
office and handed me the check. "Good luck," he said.

"Thanks. I appreciate your help."

Three days later Mutti went to the train station to
see me off. I said good-bye to Maria at home. She
showed no enthusiasm for my venture. I knew she
thought I was out of my mind.

Some Youth for Christ friends were at the station
to send me off. Their presence was a tremendous
boost because they were placing their stamp of approval on my venture. Daniel Poysti was there, too.
We had planned to travel together.

Mutti twisted a handkerchief nervously in her
hand as she boarded the train with me to say good-
bye. Her lips quivered. Daniel walked on to get us
some seats.

"Do you have to go?" she asked, hanging on to my
arm.

I held back the tears. "I'm sorry, Mutti. I'm so sorry.
Yes. There is no other way." I fought back the tears.

It was painful to disappoint someone I loved so much.

She hung on to my arm tightly. "I've got to go," I told her. "I've got to." I pulled my arm from her grasp. "Try to understand . . . I'll write."

"Please do, Traugott. Please do. Good-bye," she sobbed as the tears ran down her cheeks. She kissed me and turned toward the door to leave. Watching her get down from the train, I thought about what a disappointment I must be to her. Surely she had hoped that I would become a businessman like my dad. Never in her wildest dreams had she visualized her son's being a poor preacher boy. And I never had, either, until . . .

As my mother stood there on the platform waving and dabbing her eyes with the handkerchief, one of my Youth for Christ friends handed me an envelope.

"What is this?" I asked.

"Just something to introduce you to England."

"Thank you, friend. Thank you."

I turned and walked down the aisle. Daniel motioned for me to sit down.

"Saying good-bye is sad," he said.

"Yes, it is. I wish my mother understood why I am going. That would make it easier."

"Maybe she will—in time."

"Maybe."

Daniel Poysti was an American missionary with the Eastern European Mission organization. I had met him at a Youth for Christ rally. Later, during my stay in England, he took me to a number of evangelistic meetings.

We talked for a few minutes about the Youth for Christ work in Frankfurt. Then I remembered the envelope.

"Excuse me, please," I said, taking the envelope out of my pocket. "One of my Youth for Christ friends gave this to me when I got on the train."

Inside the envelope was a card and a British pound note. "Well, well, my first bit of British money. How thoughtful."

The card had a verse of Scripture printed on it. I read it out loud. "And we know that all things work together for good to them that love God, to them who are called according to his purpose" (Rom. 8:28, KJV).

"That's a tremendous promise," Poysti remarked.

"Yes. It is." It was my answer for that hour. The verse made my mother's sorrow and lack of understanding easier to bear. It was a wonderful promise.

Late that afternoon we boarded a ship at Ostende, Belgium, and were bound for England. The four-hour trip had passed fast because Poysti and I had so many things to talk about, so many interests in common.

The majestic White Cliffs of Dover was the first sight that greeted us as we approached the English coast. The white, shiny, marblelike wall stretched all along the coast of Dover. This beautiful scene created a tremendous surge of excitement about being in England. The future seemed as bright and majestic as the White Cliffs, illuminated by the intense light of the summer sun.

Poysti and I traveled together by train as far as London. He stayed in London, and I continued on to the college in Swansea to become the first German male student to enroll in the college, after the war.

Soon after I arrived at the college, the director introduced me to Hans Gross, a Christian Jew and the Greek professor.

"We're glad you have come our way," Mr. Gross said in German.

"Thank you," I replied in German. "I'm glad to be here."

He went on to share some general information about the school. Then he added, still speaking in German, "After you learn English, you will go on to your theological studies."

"But I already know English," I said, speaking in English. Mr. Gross and the director both looked very surprised.

"We just assumed you spoke only German," the director said.

"My mother is an Australian citizen," I explained. "I've been speaking English since I was a child."

They were very pleased and excited. "You are ready to begin your studies then," Mr. Gross said with enthusiasm. During my stay at Swansea Hans Gross was my friend as well as my Greek professor. Through this kind, gentle man, I saw another side of the Jews—the Christian side.

The first year at the college cemented and confirmed my calling. I had many opportunities to preach. Sharing Christ with others was the most exciting thing I had ever done in my life. I was totally involved in Christian service. I gave my testimony at youth rallies and sang in a quartet. And I adopted as my motto a challenge that was part of the tradition of the Bible college: "If you can't trust God at home, you can't trust him on the mission field."

On a number of occasions I applied the school motto to finances, since money was always in short supply. One time I was asked to speak at a church in a town nearly eighty miles from Swansea. I prayed about the money; but when the day came to go, there still wasn't enough money for the fare. But I decided to get on the bus and go as far as the money lasted. *Then I'll walk,* I told myself, knowing the idea was ridiculous since the distance was much too far to walk.

At the bus station in Swansea I bought a ticket to the next stop, which was about twenty-five miles away. At the next stop I bought a ticket to a town thirty miles farther. That was as far as my money would take me. *Should I go ahead and get off?* I wondered. But where would I go in a strange town? I decided to stay put until the bus driver came around. Yet it seemed so foolish.

At the next stop a middle-aged man got on the bus and sat down beside me. We nodded at each

other and exchanged greetings. He kept glancing my
way. After a few minutes he said, "Aren't you the
German friend from the college?"

"You mean at Swansea?" I asked.

"Yes."

"Yes, I am a student there. But how did you know?"

"I heard you give your testimony when I was visiting with friends in Swansea a few weeks ago. It was
very inspiring. You've been through a lot."

We were interrupted by the call "Tickets, please."
The bus driver was collecting money and tickets
from the passengers three or four rows in front of us.

I put my hand in my pocket, pretending to look for
money. My heart increased its tempo; my face grew
hot; I felt trapped. The man continued talking, but it
was difficult to concentrate on what he was saying.

"Are you going to give your testimony on Sunday?"
he asked.

"Yes . . . I plan to."

The bus driver came to the row of seats right in
front of ours.

"I know your testimony will encourage the people,"
the man continued.

"I hope so. I feel this is something the Lord wants
me to do." The conversation was making me uneasy.

The driver stood beside our seats. I looked away
and let him speak to the man first.

"Your ticket, please, sir."

He handed the man a couple of bills. "Give me two
tickets to Bath," the man said.

My mouth flew open. I couldn't believe what I was
hearing. "Isn't that so?" he asked, turning me.

"Yes," I said quietly. Bath was my last stop—the
place where I was scheduled to speak. How did he
know? I didn't ask; I just thanked him for his help.

Later on the opportunity came for me to help a
couple in their work. Gordon and Olive Bayliss did
children's work in the churches in and around Swansea. On several occasions they had expressed a need
for an easel. Harold, the American who had encour-

aged me to continue my interpreting ministry, had told me to let him know if I needed anything in children's work. He would be happy to send whatever I needed from Chicago.

In my possessions I had five American dollars that I had never converted. I had even forgotten that I had them because they were in a small box in the bottom drawer. As I thought about the easel, I felt like giving a good impression and sent the five dollars to Harold, even though I had no idea what the easel would cost. "Just spend the money in the best way possible," I told him.

Two or three weeks later the easel arrived, along with a receipt for $4.83. Harold said that he was glad to pay the postage and send the easel. I put the easel in Gordon and Olive's room. Obviously thrilled, they let everyone know what had happened. I felt a great sense of satisfaction.

The sense of satisfaction wore off quickly when I was confronted with a personal need. A few days later I took my shoes to the repair shop and was informed that the repairs would cost the equivalent of five American dollars.

"I don't know," I told the repairman, "maybe they'll last a little longer."

"If you wait any longer, they'll be beyond repair," he said, shaking his head.

"All right. Go ahead and fix them."

I walked out of the repair shop, knowing that I could not pay for the repairs. The doubts arose fast. *Was it wise to send the money,* I asked myself, *when I needed it for my shoes?*

For the first time I prayed all night. "Lord, give me some assurance that I did the right thing," I asked over and over again. "Maybe I was out of line trying to be 'Mr. Friend-in-Need' when I couldn't afford it."

As the morning dawned, I felt sure that I had an answer. After breakfast I went to check my mail, and there was a letter from Chicago. *Maybe it's from Harold,* I thought.

"Dear Traugott," the letter began. "I am attending a missions conference in Chicago and have been thinking about you and wondering how you are progressing in school. Before I return to New York, I wanted to send you this letter . . . ." Included with the letter was a check for five dollars he thought I "might be able to use." I went to the repair shop to pick up my shoes.

About a month before spring vacation my uncle, Leo, wrote a letter inviting me to spend the vacation time with him and my aunt. He sent the money for the trip along with the invitation. Uncle Leo lived on Jersey, a British island occupied by the Germans during the war. He had been a doctor in the British army and now had a thriving practice on the island.

Just before the spring vacation began I went to a Youth for Christ conference in Bournemouth, a city on the South coast. After the conference I flew on to Jersey.

From the first conversation on, it was evident that Mutti had written to Uncle Leo. He and my aunt were both kind, but he kept trying to talk me out of pursuing a preaching career.

"You should get into something that is more productive," he told me.

All week long Uncle Leo tried to be a daddy to me, giving me advice that he was sure would be helpful. He lived in high society, and he could visualize the same status for me if I "could get my head on straight."

"You have abilities and a good personality," Uncle Leo told me. "Why did you pick the ministry?"

"It's what I feel I must do, and it is something that brings great satisfaction."

He looked at me in disbelief across the breakfast table, shaking his head back and forth. "It's hard to believe that you are your father's son."

"Why?" I asked. "I'm putting my heart into something that I feel is worthwhile."

"But your selection of a lifework is not what a Vogel would pick. . . . Oh, well, let's forget about that and go for a drive. I want you to see the island."

It was a long week because we really had very little in common. I felt a great sense of relief when the time came to leave. Our parting was cool but courteous. My uncle was disappointed that he could talk no sense into me, and I was disappointed that he did not even try to understand or appreciate my goals.

But time changed things. Years later, on a visit to Germany, Uncle Leo gave me a crystal flask which was decorated with the Vogel coat of arms. My parents had given it to him as a wedding present. "That's yours," he said. "You are the only Vogel."

II
He Who Forgives

While on their honeymoon, my parents had bought some water which had come from the Jordan River and had been properly blessed by a priest. In a corner of a cabinet in the kitchen, Mutti had stored the holy water for my baptism.

In a ceremony at home shortly after my birth, a Lutheran pastor baptized me with the holy water. It was always a source of special pride for Mutti to be able to say that I had been baptized with water from the Jordan—the site of Jesus' baptism.

When I was converted I didn't think about baptism or church membership. I figured my original baptism was all I needed. But an invitation to a church in Swansea set the stage for further thought about the matter.

Just before summer vacation the pastor of Mount Pleasant Baptist Church asked me to give my testimony at a youth meeting at this large church, which was in downtown Swansea. The signals got crossed, and I arrived at the church an hour early. Unaware of the mistake, I went into the sanctuary and discovered that a baptismal service was in progress. A young lady, dressed in a white robe, was the first person to be baptized. She and the pastor, in his black robe, stood in the middle of the baptismal pool below the platform which had been removed for the ceremony.

"I baptize you, Louise Smith," the preacher began, "in the name of the Father, and of the Son, and of the Holy Spirit."

As he spoke he held his hand high and just behind her. Then he brought his hand down to cradle her head as he lowered her into the water.

"You are buried with Christ in baptism," he said as he immersed her completely, "and raised to walk in newness of life."

The lady stood straight and climbed the side stairs to get out of the pool. Following her, an older man and a young boy were baptized. The entire scene was reverent and beautiful. And the preacher's words were a personal challenge to me.

Following the baptismal service the preacher spoke about baptism. He explained what baptism stood for and why a person should be baptized. Several times he used the term "believer's baptism."

"Baptism is for those who have made a personal commitment to Christ," he affirmed. "It has no meaning apart from faith." I had never thought about baptism that way before. In fact, I had given very little thought to the subject at all.

"It is your testimony to the world that you have trusted Christ as your personal Savior and are going to live for him," he went on to say. "Every believer should be baptized."

He was very convincing, but I wanted to do some investigating of my own before I made any decision. I certainly knew that I had not been a believer at the time of my baptism. Still, why make such a big deal out of the observance? I believed in Christ—that was what mattered.

The next day I went to the college library and looked up everything available on baptism. I read what the theologians had to say about it. And I saw that many of the outstanding Christian leaders, such as Spurgeon and Moody, had been baptized as believers.

I examined three baptisms recorded in the New Testament—those of Jesus, the Ethiopian eunuch, and the Philippian jailer. They were all baptized when they were adults and understood the true meaning of faith. As I looked into the Scriptures, I became convinced that I needed to be baptized.

Through a friend at Mount Pleasant I found out when the next baptismal service would take place, and I made it a point to be there then. Again the service was impressive. At the end of the service I went to the front of the sanctuary, stood in front of the baptismal pool, and told the pastor that I wanted to say a word to the people. He was happy to let me speak.

"Now that I have found that to be baptized as a believer is a step of obedience, I want to be baptized," I told them. Many people smiled and a few nodded in agreement.

"But I want to be baptized in Germany," I continued, "as a testimony to my people."

After the service many people told me that they were happy about my decision and wished me well.

When I got home that evening I wrote to Daniel Poysti, telling him about my desire to be baptized in Germany. He wrote back soon, telling me that he would be overjoyed to baptize me. He also asked me to help him in the refugee camps during the summer months. These camps were filled with people from the Eastern Zone of Germany. A steady stream of refugees came to the camps every day.

Immediately upon my arrival in Frankfurt, I contacted Daniel Poysti and discovered that he had already made plans for the baptismal service—his first baptismal service in Europe.

"There is a mineral bath in a building downtown, and the management has agreed to let us use it," he told me. "We're going to have people baptized from three nations—America, Russia, and Germany."

"That sounds great," I said. "When will it be?"

"Sunday evening at seven o'clock. Invite your friends."

I thought about Mutti and Maria but decided not to say anything. They wouldn't come, I knew. I had invited them to services many times, but they had always had excuses.

Before a small group of friends, Daniel baptized fifteen of us in a service that was conducted in three languages. To me the service not only pictured my personal commitment to Christ; it also symbolized a common bond that can exist among people of all languages. We were all united in Christ.

Mutti was sitting in the living room reading when I came in that evening. I sat down to chat with her for a minute.

"What do you have in the bundle?" she asked.

"My wet clothes," I said.

"Wet clothes! Traugott, what happened? Did you fall in the river?"

I looked straight into her eyes and said, "I was baptized this evening."

"Baptized?" she said with great surprise. "But why?"

"Because I felt it was something I should do."

"Was this really necessary?"

"Yes, I think so."

"But don't you remember that you were baptized as a baby?"

"Yes, but that meant nothing to me."

"But it *was* meaningful. You were baptized with holy water from the Jordan."

"Mutti, you don't understand. I really believe in Christ now, and that's why I was baptized. I wanted to tell the world that I'm going to live for him."

"You seem to go out of your way to hurt me. It all seems so unnecessary," she added with despair in her voice.

"But it is necessary, Mutti." I got up, walked over to the sofa, and sat beside her. "Why don't you give your life to Christ and let him forgive your sins and start you out in a new life?" I asked as I put my arm around her shoulder.

Quickly she turned around to face me. "Forgive my

sins? I've done nothing wrong," she replied defensively. "But how could God let me lose two husbands? I've suffered so much." Her voice cracked.

"Mutti, you've got it wrong. God didn't do it. And when you give your life to him, he gives you so much. He makes life so rich and full."

"That's impossible."

She didn't know what I was talking about, and nothing I could say would make her understand. This was just one of the many times I talked to her about choosing the Christ life for herself. It was painful to disappoint her, but I was determined to continue in the life I had chosen—even if my own mother thought I was going off the deep end.

I stayed with Daniel Poysti and did mission work in the German and Slavic refugee camps the summer after my first year in Bible college. The refugee camps seemed to be the greatest need our country had at that time. It was easy for me to identify with these displaced persons, for I, too, had been a refugee. I knew what it was to be without a home and without enough money to secure even the necessities of life. I knew what it was to face the future without a glimmer of hope.

Over the loudspeakers in the camps, we invited everyone to the worship services. Poysti, who was a son of missionaries to Russia, preached to the people. Often I translated his message into German from English.

On one occasion we had a close call. A group of Kalmuks were in the crowd near the back of the building. For a while these people of Islamic background listened to Poysti. Then, suddenly, in the middle of the sermon, they stood up as a group and began shouting. Standing just behind them, I spotted the knives sticking out of their pockets. I ran out the back door to get the camp police. When they walked in, the Kalmuks sat down.

Most of the experiences in the camps were challenging in a positive way, and these experiences cemented my plans for the immediate future. In the fall of 1952 I went back to college determined to join the refugee work after graduation. The people in the camps were so responsive to the gospel, and the need was so great.

During the school year, the president of the Eastern European Mission came to the Bible college to interview me for full-time mission work among the refugees. I was accepted and began that work the next summer after graduation. My first assignment was at Solingen in West Germany, where Daniel Poysti was the field director. We had regular worship services in the camps, along with a program of follow-up to new Christians.

In the spring I attended a German Youth for Christ conference in Siegen. At that meeting I saw a young nurse named Holdine Rupp, who worked in a large hospital in Berlin. We met informally and talked about the refugee work in Berlin. Then, early in 1954, a trustee of the Eastern European Mission came from California to see the refugee work. He asked me to show him the camp work in West Germany and insisted that we go to Berlin, although that was not part of our territory.

When we arrived at the camp, we checked in first with the proper authorities and then went to a circular bunker which had been used for an air-raid shelter during the war. It served as living quarters for male refugees. We talked with the men briefly and invited them to the worship services that evening. When we walked out of the bunker I saw a familiar face, but I couldn't remember the girl's name.

"Hello," I said, smiling as I walked up to her. "Remember me?"

She looked surprised and puzzled.

"I'm Birdy."

She still looked blank.

"We met at the Youth for Christ conference."

"Oh . . . yes," she said. "I remember. It was at Siegen, wasn't it?"

"That's right. But I'm sorry; I don't remember your name."

"Holdine," she said with an enthusiastic smile.

"What are you doing here?" I asked.

"What do you think? I'm working."

"Full-time?"

"No, just in my spare time. I still work at the hospital."

"Will you be at the services tonight?"

"Yes, I will."

"I'll see you then. All right?"

"All right."

The trustee left, and I stayed in Berlin for about two months, conducting services on a regular basis at the camp. Holdine and I began dating right away. She was fun to be with, and our goals in life were so compatible. She sincerely wanted to do God's will. Naturally, it was a big disappointment when word came that I would have to return to Solingen.

"I hate to leave," I told Holdine after the camp services one evening as we sat in a restaurant drinking coffee and eating dessert. "This has been a wonderful two months for me."

"For me, too," she said softly.

We talked for a long time about the experiences of the two months. The time had gone by so fast because we had been together. We finished our dessert and coffee and went out to catch a streetcar. While we waited we stood facing each other, holding hands.

"Will you serve the Lord with me from now on?" I asked.

"That would be nice."

I leaned over and kissed her on the cheek. And there on that street corner, unaware of the other people waiting for the same car, we promised each other that we would get married and serve the Lord together.

Shortly before leaving Berlin I met another lady who also greatly influenced my life. The camp director asked me to pick her up at a house across town. He explained that she was a Dutch lady who was going to speak to the refugees in the evening services. I wondered what important thing a lady would have to say to the refugees.

"Who is she?" I asked the director.

"Corrie ten Boom," he replied.

The name meant nothing to me. "Why have you invited her to speak?"

"She has something to say that will help these people," he said. And then almost as an afterthought, added, "She may even touch your heart."

"Maybe so," I said. "It's just unusual for a woman to speak in the worship services."

When I arrived at the house, Miss ten Boom's hostess invited me in. Miss ten Boom was seated on the sofa.

"Miss ten Boom, I'm Traugott Vogel from the refugee camp. I'll take you there."

"I'm very glad to know you," she said, standing up. "It's so nice of you to come to get me." She gave me a warm handshake.

On the way to the camp she told me a little about herself—how she had worked in the Dutch underground and what she was doing now. But she wanted to know something about me and how I happened to be involved in the refugee work.

"It's a great need," I told her. "And it's something that I feel the Lord wants me to do right now."

"That's true contentment," she said, "when you're doing what the Lord wants you to do, no matter what obstacles come along." She knew what she was talking about, I found out later.

In the evening services Corrie ten Boom related many of her experiences in a German concentration camp. She told of deep spiritual experiences, deeper than I had ever experienced or heard about. One experience stood out among the others. It dealt with the request of a lady whose son was a former SS guard. At the time of the request, the lady's son was in the same prison that Miss ten Boom had been confined in during the war. The lady wanted her to visit with her son and encourage him. "He did some terrible things in the war," she told Miss ten Boom. "But he has come to Jesus."

When Miss ten Boom went to visit the lady's son, she recognized him as one who had mistreated her while she was a prisoner. Inside her came the question, *Your sins are forgiven, but is it that easy for me to forgive?* The question was followed by an affirmation: *God forgives, and it is all over; it's in the past, forgotten. If God forgives, then I must forgive.* Miss ten Boom tried to get a pardon for the man from the Queen of Holland.

This lady's struggle with forgiveness made a deep impression on me. I, too, had a problem with forgiveness—a problem I had refused to admit, even to myself. Her words made the problem nag at me—over and over.

Shortly after Miss ten Boom's visit to Berlin, word came that the western headquarters for the Eastern European Mission had been moved to Frankfurt. I had a few days' leave before reporting for my new assignment.

"What are you going to do with the free days?" Poysti asked me.

"I think I'll go south to Bavaria."

"I'm going to Munich. Want to go there?"

"Yes. That will be fine. There's lots to do in that city. I'll stay there overnight, then go to Oberstaufen, the site of my evacuated school."

"OK. I'll pick you up at your apartment at eight in the morning."

"All right."

On the way to Bavaria I kept thinking about my experiences in Berlin. I reviewed Corrie ten Boom's words over and over. "God forgives, and it is all over."

Is it all over? I asked myself. *Jesus has forgiven so*

much, but I am not willing to forgive so little. I forgive when it is easy.

"You're so deep in thought," Poysti observed, as we rode along.

"Oh, I was just thinking about everything that happened in Berlin." I mentioned Corrie ten Boom and how she had come to the point where she could forgive. Poysti and I talked about the obligation to forgive, but he didn't know what I was getting at.

"Can't you just forgive someone without saying anything to that person?" I asked.

"It just depends, but most of the time forgiveness should be communicated if you have the opportunity and if the offended person will listen. Do you have a particular example in mind?"

"Not really. Miss ten Boom's visit just made me think about it."

"Often the person who won't forgive suffers more than the person he refuses to forgive," Poysti observed.

"I guess that's right. It eats at you, doesn't it?"

"Yes, it does."

Poysti let me off near Oberstaufen, and I rented a room in a large house that had been converted into a hotel. The two men who had killed my father were on my mind constantly.

They killed a civilian, but they've never been prosecuted, I thought as I ate the evening meal. *They should pay for that. And they should pay for Vati's death.*

I felt guilty for hating them so, but I couldn't be sure that my hatred for them was all wrong. *Justice should be done,* I was convinced. *That's not anti-Christian.*

After dinner I went to the sparsely furnished upstairs bedroom. In one corner was a single bed with an iron frame. In front of the gable window stood a small table with a straight-backed chair pushed under it. These items were the extent of the furnishings.

I got my Bible out of my suitcase, pulled out the chair, and sat down at the table. For a few minutes I stared out the small window. The scene was peaceful with the trees blowing gently.

Soon darkness descended on the area, and I turned on the bare ceiling light so that I could read my Bible. I turned to 1 John 4. "He who does not love does not know God; for God is love. . . . If any one says, 'I love God,' and hates his brother, he is a liar" (vv. 8, 20, RSV). Over and over I read the verses that spoke to my condition. The words penetrated more deeply than ever before.

As I read and began to reevaluate my situation, I was confronted with the truth that there was something that stood between me and God—a block, an obstacle.

I must face up to, it, I told myself over and over. *But how?* I asked.

Jacob and Esau came to mind. The barrier between brothers had created a barrier between man and God. And Jacob had to act to break down the barrier.

For two or three hours—how long I'm not sure—I prayed and read my Bible. Gradually I came to the realization that I had not opened up all the way to God. I had done so many things to serve him, but one part of me had not surrendered. In all the time I had been a Christian, I had not allowed God to speak to me about my attitude toward my father's killers.

When I fell asleep I knew that I must surrender the Austrians to God. I had to let him take care of the situation. I had to face the killers.

In the morning I walked through Oberstaufen to the site of the evacuated school. Standing there before the hotel that had once served as a dormitory, I remembered the marching, the war games, and the regimented life. I remembered the jam and crackers, too.

That afternoon I boarded a train for Reutte, Austria, wishing there was another way. During the trip I thought about the treatment my family had endured in Austria—the subtle hostility, the acts of violence, and the murder. It was all a nightmare; there was nothing pleasant to remember.

Maybe I'm digging up something that should stay buried, I told myself. There seemed to be no real reason to revive the past. What could be accomplished? When I saw the marker—"Leaving Germany, Entering Austria"—a strange feeling erupted within. I began to review the details of the killing. The gun fired, and the general fell backward. My father fell on his face. I ran to help him. I could hear Mutti and Maria cry. I saw the coffins.

"Why? Why?" I whispered. "He could be living today if it weren't for them." Then the thought flashed across my mind, *But maybe he would be in prison like so many other SS officers.*

That thought was replaced by another. *But maybe not . . . he was a good man.*

Then I thought about Jesus. *Maybe I would never have known him if my father had lived.* Strangely, the thought did not bring peace. It only increased the tension.

In Reutte I walked around the downtown area for a while. I passed the corner where Vati had stood with fellow officers the day before his death. I could hear them joking and smiling. I caught a bus for Bach near the same place where Vati and I had boarded a truck on that day of reunion.

Bach was as beautiful as ever with the thick green foliage and tree-covered mountains. This town, which had grown considerably, was now an attraction for German tourists. I went out to the area where our lodge was located and found that it was occupied. I sat down beside a tree across the street and looked at it and mused. We had spent many vacations there. Memories of those vacations came to mind as I glanced beyond the lodge to the road that circled behind it.

"The murderers stood on that road," I whispered. I got up and headed down the street in the direction

of the home of one of the men. Slowly I walked up to
the door and knocked. An old man answered the
knock—the man's father, I assumed.

"Where is your son?" I asked.

"Who are you?" he responded with a puzzled
look on his face.

"I'm Traugott Vogel," I replied in a soft tone.

He looked surprised and uneasy. "Vogel . . . oh,
you're the doctor's son. I didn't recognize you. You
look different. You've been gone a long time, haven't
you?"

"Yes, quite a while."

"Why do you want him?"

"I just want to greet him."

"Greet him? Why?"

"I was just passing through and thought I would
stop by."

"I didn't know you were friends."

"We weren't, but I did know him," I said. "I . . ."

"Dad, who is it?"

The man turned to talk to a woman who appeared
to be in her late twenties. She was pregnant.

"Just a man from Reutte, asking about the tractor."

"Oh," she said and went to the back of the house.

He turned back to me, looking quite serious. "Vo-
gel," he began, stepping outside and closing the door.
"I know why you're here. You're no friend of my son.
Sit down for a minute and let me talk to you."

We both sat down on the edge of the narrow porch.
He continued to speak.

"We've always felt you would come back someday
to settle the matter, but we hoped you would forget
the past."

"But . . ."

"Just let me tell you a few things first," he interrupted. "Then you can talk. There are some things
you don't know. I am quite aware of my son's reputation. He did a lot of terrible things in his youth.
But he's married now and has settled down."

"Oh," I responded.

"The girl is not from around here. She knows nothing of the incident at your lodge. We felt there was no good reason to tell her."

"You mean you let her marry a guy like that with her eyes closed?" I demanded.

"He's different now."

"Are you sure?"

"Yes, I'm sure. So why don't you forget about everything and go on your way?"

"But I can't. I've got to see him."

"Why? It will only revive the old hate. Go on and forget it."

"I'm sorry, I can't. I must see him."

"It will do no good."

"Yes, it will help me and him, too, I think."

"Help him—how?"

"Just tell me where he is, and don't worry. I'm not going to hurt him."

"Why bother seeing him then?"

"Trust me, please. I give you my word. I won't hurt him. I'm a changed man, too. Please, where is he?"

The man stood up and walked down the steps to the grass. "All right, I'll tell you where he is. But if you hurt him, I'll be after you."

"Don't worry. I'm on a different kind of mission."

"Oh?" he said with a puzzled look on his face. He pointed down the hill. "He's just beyond those bushes, mowing the grass near the river."

"Thank you, sir," I said and headed in that direction.

The man stood by the front door for a few minutes and watched me go down the hill to the river. I looked back once to see an extremely concerned look on his face.

With each step I thought about turning back. *Why dig up the past?* I wondered. *It will do no good.*

I spotted the man sitting near the bank with a scythe beside him. He was resting.

Forget it, Traugott, I told myself as I came near the man. *Forget it.* I stepped on some dry twigs when I turned to leave. The man turned around.

"Why, hello," he said. "I didn't even hear you coming down the hill. What are you doing?" he asked, making conversation. He was a big man with the complexion and manner of a rugged farmer. His looks matched his reputation.

"I've just come to talk to you."

"Oh . . . Who are you?"

"Traugott Vogel."

"Vogel? That name sounds familiar. Do you live around here?"

"I used to."

"Oh? Where?"

"Up the street. At the hunting lodge." I pointed in that direction.

"Are you the doctor's son?" he asked with a slight nervousness developing in his voice.

"That's right."

A look of disgust covered his face. "Why have you come?"

"I wanted to talk with you."

"I thought you might come sometime," he said, turning his head to break eye contact. "To see your lodge," he added. "Someone lives there now, you know."

"I didn't really come back to see the lodge. I wanted to talk with you."

"Why dig up the past? The war is behind us."

"It's not completely over, for me, anyway." I put my hand in my pants' pocket.

"What are you doing!" the man exclaimed, jumping to his feet.

"What do you mean?" I asked.

"What do you have in your pocket?" he demanded.

"Oh, nothing. That's just a habit."

"All right, get on with why you came here. I want to get this job done," he said impatiently.

"Let's both sit down, and I'll tell you why I'm here."

"All right," he agreed.

I sat there for a moment, trying to find the words. Finally the words formed. "I've hated you all these years," I began slowly, "for having a part in the death of my father."

"I don't know what you're talking about," he said defensively. "I had no part. You're crazy!"

"There were many who knew about you and your friend," I said, pointing in the direction of the home of his partner in the killing.

"You're crazy," he said again, his voice still betraying a nervous quiver.

I didn't push him any further. He could never admit anything because of the killing of the general's wife. For killing a civilian he could pay dearly.

"It doesn't matter now," I assured him. "I didn't come to turn you in."

"Then why did you come?"

"I wanted to come to the place that brought me so much tragedy."

"But why? Why keep dwelling on the past? The war is over."

"Because I'm a different person now."

"What do you mean?" he asked, obviously puzzled by the trend of the conversation.

I told him that I had dedicated my life to Christ and that I was a missionary among the refugees. He showed little emotion as he listened to my story.

"Are you a priest?" he asked when I had finished.

"No, I'm with a Protestant interdenominational organization." I explained a little about the work of our mission.

"But have you come here just to tell me that? Why would I be interested? I'm not a Protestant."

"No. That's not the only reason I've come. I came to ask you a favor."

"A favor?"

"Yes. Will you do me a favor?"

"I don't know. What is it?"

"Will you forgive me for hating you all these years?" I blurted out.

"Forgive you?" he questioned, shaking his head back and forth. "You must be kidding," he added, half laughing.

"No, I'm not. I really mean it. I've hated you a lot, and I'm sorry. I've been wrong, and I want you to forgive me."

"But you haven't hurt me."

"Yes, I have, and I'm sorry. Will you forgive me?"

The man looked trapped. "If it will make you feel better, I will," he said, with a tone of resignation evident in his voice.

"Thank you," I said quietly. "That means more to me than you can ever know."

He gave me a funny look, still trying to figure out what was happening.

"Will you tell your partner I came?"

"He's dead."

"Oh, I'm sorry."

"He died several years ago."

I stood up. "I must leave now," I told him.

He stood up, and I held my hand out to him. Reluctantly, he returned the gesture.

"Thank you," I said and turned to begin the climb up the hill to the road. At the top of the hill I turned around to see that he was still watching me. I waved to him; he waved back; and I went on my way.

What peace I felt as I walked to the downtown area of Bach! A heavy burden had been lifted from my shoulders. At last I had forgiven. The countryside was more beautiful than ever, and the expressions on the faces of the people I passed were pleasant. I could smile first and greet the Austrians.

12
What's in a Name?

The meeting with the Austrian inaugurated a new period in my life. From that point, I seemed to be going forward in a new way. A dimension of joy that I didn't know was missing had been added to my Christian life. I returned to Frankfurt and resumed my work with the refugees.

Some months later, on the invitation of Dawson Trotman, I went to the Billy Graham 1954 London Crusade. This was the first time I had ever been in such a large meeting, and it was a tremendous thrill to see so many people respond to the call of Christ.

In January of 1955 Holdine came to Frankfurt on her way to London. An English family was sponsoring her so that she could go to England and learn the language. During her short stay in Frankfurt we became engaged. And, in keeping with German custom, I placed the ring on her left hand. Later, during the marriage ceremony, I would remove that same ring from her left hand and place it on her right hand —also according to German custom. At the train station we said good-bye.

"Fourteen months is a long time to be separated," I told her.

"Maybe you'll get to come to London for the Billy Graham Crusade."

"I hope so. Anyway, keep care of yourself and learn the English."

"I will. You keep care of yourself, too."

"I wish we could get married now."

"I do, too; but I need to get this training. The opportunity may not come again."

"That's right, but I'll miss you so. I could teach you English."

"I can't change my plans now."

"I know."

"I'll miss you."

As the train pulled out of the station, we both had tears in our eyes. But it did seem she should go to England for the training.

Soon after Holdine's visit to Frankfurt, an invitation came for me to go to the United States. It came from Dean Hamilton, a retired pastor in California. He was the founder of the Fellowship of Philip, a group that emphasized personal witnessing.

"You will remember that you interpreted for me at the missionary conference in Berlin," the letter went. "And I also heard you speak at that conference."

He went on to say that he would like for me to come to the United States to look at the work of his organization and to speak in a number of cities. An acceptance letter was in the mail the day after the invitation arrived. Being invited to America was like a dream come true.

"I would love to come to America," I told him, "and am grateful that you have asked me." In the correspondence that developed as a result of the planned trip, Hamilton indicated that he would like for me to continue his work. He was eighty years old and, of course, didn't feel that he could stay in the work much longer.

"I will consider your proposal," I told him. "It's something that I would like to do."

When I told Mutti about the invitation, her response was different from her attitude when I went to Wales.

"What are you going to do?" she asked.

"I'm going to share my testimony with the people and look at the work of this Christian organization."

"How long will you be gone?"

"About six months."

"Don't decide to stay there," she chuckled. "I want you near. But it is a marvelous opportunity. You will have so many new experiences and see so many new sights."

Mutti would not admit it, but her feelings toward my vocational choice were changing. She was a little proud. Her enthusiasm did have boundaries, though.

"Oh, by the way. I was looking through the books we saved from the bombing, and I found the Bible."

"What Bible?" she asked.

"The one you and Vati got when you were married."

"Oh, I had forgotten about that."

"Would you mind if I took it for my own?"

"I have no use for it. Take it."

"Thank you, Mutti," I said quietly, wishing in a way that she did want it.

With relative ease, compared to the difficulty of getting permission to go to the Bible college, I secured a visa to stay in the United States for six months.

A few weeks later I got the chance to tell Holdine the news in person. In May I went to the Billy Graham Wembly Crusade. Holdine and I were together a lot during the week, and we talked about the trip more than anything else.

"What can this trip mean?" she asked as we drank tea in a restaurant after one of the crusade meetings.

"Who knows?" I said. "I just feel that it is a great opportunity."

We were both very excited, but neither of us considered the possibility that one day we would be in the United States as permanent residents. That was something beyond us.

I went back to Germany by way of Paris, where Billy Graham had a crusade in June. I arrived in Frankfurt just in time to prepare for another crusade, which was held later on in the month. In that meeting I served as an interpreter for Cliff Barrows.

On the first of August I severed my ties with the Eastern European Mission and was on my way to

America within a month. Mutti went to the train station with me. "Have a good time," she told me. "Maybe I'll go there someday." The next year she did go to the US to visit friends.

Holdine and I met in London, and she took me to the boat in Southampton to leave for the US. I sailed on the S.S. *America,* sister ship to the *United States.* The people on the ship were pleasant and interested in why I was going to America. But the weather was miserable.

In the second day out a storm developed in the North Atlantic. The ship tossed back and forth. I got sick—sicker than I can ever remember. I longed for home. I spent most of the trip in my room trying to recover with the aid of the prescriptions the doctor gave me. This aspect of the trip had not been included in my dreaming.

I did recover from my seasickness; and on September 27, 1955, Holdine's birthday, the S.S. *America* pulled into New York harbor.

The sight of the Statue of Liberty overshadowed everything. It was so majestic, towering above us. I remembered two of the lines inscribed on the bronze tablet affixed to the pedestal that held the statue:

> *Give me your tired, your poor,*
> *Your huddled masses yearning to be free.*

"It's wonderful, wonderful," I exclaimed to the group at my table. Very few of them were so impressed. For some the inscription was old hat because they had seen the statue many times. Some did not even look up from their evening meal to view the scene.

Soon after the ship pulled into the harbor, a bellboy entered the dining room and came straight to our table. He held a newspaper in his hand with a piece of paper wrapped around it. He stood at the end of the table to address us.

"Mr. Vogel?" he questioned.

"I'm Vogel," I said, motioning for him to come to me.

"This is for you," he said, handing me the newspaper.

"For me?" I questioned. "Thank you. But why me? Who sent it?"

"Look at the wrapper," he replied and went on his way.

I removed the wrapped and read the brief message out loud: "To Mr. Vogel. Compliments of the pilot."

"Well, how do you rate?" one man asked.

"There must be something in it about you," the man's wife added.

Everyone at the table was curious and anxious to help me scan the paper. We took the paper apart by sections and, by twos, scanned the contents carefully.

"I didn't find anything," one remarked.

"Me either."

"Do you want to look for yourself?" someone asked. "We may not know what to look for."

"No. All of you would have found it. There's nothing in this paper about me." I said, reassembling the paper and setting it aside.

"Surely someone will clear things up," one lady suggested. "Who is the pilot, anyway? Do you know anyone in the United States?"

"Not that I know of," I replied. "It is possible, though. My grandmother was married in New York, but she didn't live here. Maybe someone just likes Germans," I added with a chuckle. "They *are* nice people."

A few minutes later a man in uniform came into the dining room. A steward led him to our table.

"Who is Mr. Vogel?" he asked.

"I am."

He stretched out his hand and said, "Welcome to the United States of America."

I stood up to take his hand. "Thank you, sir, but why such an honor?"

"I'm Roy Wood."

"Roy Wood?" I questioned. The name meant nothing to me.

All eyes were on us as Roy explained that he was a distant relative of my Grandmother Ratazzi.

"Your mother wrote, telling me about your visit."

"I wonder why she never told me about you."

"No telling."

"It was lucky you guided the ship in, wasn't it?"

"Yes. This is my regular assignment."

Roy Wood's greeting added to the already great excitement that I felt about being in the US. He invited me to stay in his home and offered any assistance he could to make my stay more pleasant.

After the short visit with Roy and his family, I preached in New York and went to a meeting in connection with the Fellowship of Philip. My next stop was Washington, D.C. Abraham Vereide, Secretary General of the International Christian Leadership, had invited me to speak to a distinguished group at the headquarters for this organization. At that time Vereide was responsible for the presidential prayer breakfasts. Washington, D.C., with all its monuments and gracious people, was very impressive. And my treatment there was royal.

Along the way to my final destination of Burbank, California, I preached in Detroit, Chicago, Denver, Albuquerque, and Flagstaff, Arizona. With Burbank as our base of operation, I worked for several months with Dean Hamilton and the Fellowship of Philip. In this work I preached in churches representing more than fifteen denominations.

Near the end of my six-month stay, Daniel Poysti arranged for me to preach in the First Baptist Church of Atlantic City. The church gave me an official license to preach; and shortly thereafter, I was formally appointed as a missionary to Buchen, Germany. The appointment was a joint venture of the church and a missionary organization.

On April 1, I arrived in Germany and immediately contacted Holdine. She had returned to Berlin while

I was in America. We began making plans for our wedding. Because of our many American friends, we had invitations printed in both English and German. On April 27 we were married at a church in Berlin, and the two of us went to Buchen as missionaries. Our major responsibility was to oversee established work in the refugee camps. We spent three days in the camp and three days in a retreat for refugee children. We also did some relief ministry, such as providing clothing.

For more than a year Holdine and I worked together among the refugees. But we knew the work could not last indefinitely. A friend who was in the know made us aware of the situation.

"Eventually," my friend said, "the Russians are going to do something to stop the flow of refugees from the Eastern Zone of Germany. It's draining off the population."

"How do you think they'll do it?" I asked.

He didn't know or he wouldn't tell me all he knew. But his information was reliable; and because of what he told me, I began to explore other possibilities for service. The final decision was based on which nation I would serve.

I felt torn between two nations. I had been converted among the Americans, and my church membership was still in America at the church in Atlantic City. Always I had served under a mission organization sponsored by the Americans. But I was German.

"Maybe we could serve the Germans better under the Germans rather than under an American mission organization," I suggested to Holdine as we considered our future.

"That may be better," she agreed, "but it is good to work with the Americans."

We both agonized over the decision. We hated to break ties with our American friends. Finally we decided to join the Germans with the idea of maintaining contact with the Americans. But we determined always to leave our hearts open for what God wanted us to do. We did not know where we would be a year later, or even a month later, for that matter. We would follow the Lord one step at a time.

In the summer of 1958 we joined a German Baptist church in Heeren, Germany. That fall Holdine stayed with our two young sons, Emanuel and Michael; I moved to Hamburg. I planned to enter the theological seminary for German Baptists located in that city. A lady from Ocean City, New Jersey, who heard that I was going to the seminary, helped me a lot along the way.

In 1960 I received my diploma from the serminary and became pastor of a church in Hamburg. For eight years I served the German Baptists primarily as a pastor and for a brief time as a home missionary in Belgium. During that time our family was completed —Dolores and then Johanna were born.

Opportunities to interpret continued to come my way. In the fall of 1961 a friend from the Pocket Testament League called me.

"Traugott, are you free September 21?" he asked.

I checked my calendar.

"Sure. Sure. What do you have in mind?"

"Captain Fuchida is coming to town, and he needs an interpreter. You know who he is, don't you?"

"Certainly. He led the attack on Pearl Harbor. I've heard a lot about him. He has an outstanding Christian testimony."

"He's going to speak in the military chapel. I'll pick you up around six and take you there."

"Fine."

As I interpreted for Fuchida I was totally involved in the testimony. Once again I was impressed and amazed with how God can change a life.

While we labored among the Germans, we kept in contact with our American friends. From time to time they came by to visit; and on special occasions I spoke in the chapels on the military bases.

A German pastor's conference set the stage for a

new development in my life. At that conference I met Lewis Krause, fraternal representative of the Southern Baptists to the German Baptists. We roomed together and talked about the Baptist work in Germany.

In October Krause called me at my church in Treysa. "Have you ever thought of pastoring an American church?" he asked.

"No, not really," I replied.

"There's a church in Bitburg that was started by a group of GIs this past summer. There are a few Germans in the congregation, but it's mostly Americans."

"Is it a military church?" I asked.

"No, it's not connected with the military, although there are many military people in the congregation. It's in an area where there are no Baptist churches of any kind. They need a pastor."

"I just haven't thought about an American church."

"Well, would you go and preach for them one Sunday?"

"Yes, I can do that."

On the last Sunday in November, Holdine and I traveled to Bitburg. The enthusiastic spirit of the people was thrilling. We both liked what we saw and felt. On the way home we stopped in Wiesbaden to talk to Lewis Krause. Mrs. Krause greeted us warmly and asked us to come in and chat for a while.

"How did you like it?" Lewis asked us as we sat in their living room drinking coffee.

"Real fine bunch of people," I replied.

"Very nice," Holdine agreed.

"Would you want to go there as pastor?" he asked.

"I don't know. I just don't know. The idea is so new to me."

All the way home Holdine and I talked about the possibilities of the Bitburg church. "But we really don't have a decision to make," we decided, because the church had not made a decision about us. A couple of weeks later that decision came. The Bitburg church sent a deacon to extend a call to me to come to the church as pastor.

Again I was torn between serving Germans or serving Americans. In a way, it seemed a little foolish to even consider becoming pastor of the church because no German had ever pastored an English-speaking Baptist church in Germany. It was one thing to work alongside Americans and under their supervision. It was another matter to be the main leader of a congregation. As I wrestled through the decision, a pastor friend came by Treysa.

"You can do it," he told me. "Your English is good, and you know something about how the Americans think."

"I'm not sure I know enough," I told him. "But the church does offer a real challenge."

"Yes, it's in an area that has possibilities for growth. And the people really seem to want to do something."

"It's up to you," Holdine told me, but she leaned toward accepting the call.

With a lot of uneasiness and with a strong feeling that we should go to Bitburg, I wrote a letter to Hardy Nall, chairman of the pulpit committee. As I mailed the letter a sense of relief came over me. I didn't really know why. But as I look back, I can see that the decision was a significant part of getting the matter settled about my direction in life.

Mr. Nall responded to my acceptance with a telephone call.

"We knew you were the man for the job," he told me. "When can you come?"

"I should be able to move there within two months."

"Fine. We'll keep in touch and help you in any way we can."

"Oh, you'll go to America one day," many people said after I told my congregation about the decision to go to Bitburg.

"I'm simply going to Bitburg to work with the

Americans," I told them. I knew that I could not leave my mother in Germany. Although she had visited America and liked it, I knew Germany would always be her home. So I didn't think seriously about their suggestion.

Within a few months I had become thoroughly immersed in the work of the English-speaking churches that were organized under the banner of the European Baptist Convention. In 1968-69 I served as vice-president of the Convention; and in 1972 I brought greetings from the European Baptist Convention to the Southern Baptist Convention, which was meeting in Philadelphia, Pennsylvania. This greeting was part of a six-week tour to the United States that had been arranged and sponsored by former deacons of the church in Bitburg who had returned to the States.

Holdine and I liked working with Americans, so we decided to look around while we were in the US. Homer Franklin, a former Bitburg deacon, and his pastor, Jack Clinkscales, from Big Spring, Texas, got the ball rolling. When I preached at the First Baptist Church in Wichita Falls, Texas, they came to see me to ask how I felt about the possibility of coming to America as a permanent resident.

We are open to the idea," I told him, "if we feel that it is the right thing to do." And that's how we left the matter.

Shortly after we returned to Germany we discovered that my mother had cancer. She was seventy-nine years old. Eight months later, in March, 1973, she died, still not understanding why I chose the Christ way of life. I mourned her death as anyone would mourn a beloved mother, but I mourned her death even more because there were no more opportunities to try to help her understand. She, too, could have known the joy of serving Christ.

Within a few months, a series of events began that ultimately resulted in setting our direction in life, at least for the near future. Emanuel was the main person in the first event. During the summer an

American friend told us that his parents would like to have Emanuel go to live with them in the US. There he would attend high school. Of course, Emanuel was delighted to accept the invitation. Before the end of summer, he was on his way to Huntsville, Texas. In September he enrolled in high school.

Then Jack Clinkscales wrote early in 1974: "There is a church in Sterling City, Texas, that needs a pastor. Are you interested? If you are, I will recommend you."

I was interested and told him so.

Within a few weeks Howard Cudd, chairman of the pulpit committee of the church, called and invited me to preach to the committee. I came to Sterling City, preached, and stayed with friends while the church made the decision. While I waited I got in touch with Emanuel. He loved America and did not want to go back to Germany.

One week after I preached, Mr. Cudd called me in New Mexico. "We want you to come as our pastor," he said. "We feel that you are the right person for our church. . . ."

"I appreciate your confidence. And I'll write you when I decide."

That afternoon I flew to Atlanta for a speaking engagement, praying about the decision as I had for some time. Earlier I had placed a call to Bitburg, Germany. Holdine answered the phone.

"Darling, they've called us."

"Wonderful!" she exclaimed. "What do we do now?"

I told her to call the chairman of the deacons and tell him that we were going to the United States. Before I went to bed I wrote my letter of acceptance to the First Baptist Church of Sterling City, Texas. A few days later I returned to Germany to bring my family to the United States.

Securing visas was the first item of business. When I applied for my visa in Frankfort, the American consul had difficulty pronouncing my name.

"How do you say your first name?" he asked. "Is it 'True-got'"?

"No, it's Trow as in cow—Trow-got."

"That's a hard name to pronounce. You might want to consider changing it since you plan to stay in the US."

"No, I don't want to do that," I replied quickly. "The name means something to me. As long as you have 'Trust God' on your coins, I'll keep it as my name."

Often I have thought, *If I had not lived up to my name and trusted God, where would I be now?*

Surely under the SS shadow, comes the speedy and frightening realization.

ABOUT THE AUTHORS

TRAUGOTT VOGEL, born in Heidelberg, Germany, is the son of the late Karl Traugott Vogel, an SS officer. At Traugott's birth, his father was a successful industrialist. His mother was the daughter of a consul to Australia. After World War II, when employment was closed to him because of his Nazi past, Vogel turned to the American military. While working with the Americans, he became involved in the Youth for Christ movement and did YMCA work in his spare time. For a number of years he worked among the Germans in the refugee camps and in German churches. In 1968 he became pastor of an English-speaking Baptist church in Bitburg, Germany. Since 1974 he has served the First Baptist Church of Sterling City, Texas.

SHIRLEY STEPHENS, who joins Traugott Vogel in telling his story, is a free-lance writer living in Nashville, Tennessee. She has years of writing and editing experience.

Heartwarming Books
of
Faith and Inspiration

☐	11710	**THE GOSPEL ACCORDING TO PEANUTS** Robert L. Short	$1.50
☐	2568	**BLESS THIS HOUSE** Anita Bryant	$1.50
☐	10891	**THE ENCHANTED BARN** Grace Livingston Hill	$1.50
☐	2714	**LOVE AND LAUGHTER** Marjorie Holmes	$1.50
☐	10866	**THE GREATEST MIRACLE IN THE WORLD** Og Mandino	$1.75
☐	2866	**THE WOMAN AT THE WELL** Dale Evans Rogers	$1.50
☐	12009	**THE GREATEST SALESMAN IN THE WORLD** Og Mandino	$1.95
☐	2936	**I'VE GOT TO TALK TO SOMEBODY, GOD** Marjorie Holmes	$1.75
☐	7712	**HOW TO TALK TO GOD WHEN YOU AREN'T FEELING RELIGIOUS** Charles Smith	$1.25
☐	10210	**WHO AM I GOD?** Marjorie Holmes	$1.75
☐	10509	**THE TASTE OF NEW WINE** Keith Miller	$1.75
☐	12066	**TWO FROM GALILEE** Marjorie Holmes	$1.95
☐	11180	**LIGHTHOUSE** Eugenia Price	$1.75
☐	11189	**NEW MOON RISING** Eugenia Price	$1.75
☐	11291	**THE LATE GREAT PLANET EARTH** Hal Lindsey	$1.95
☐	11140	**REFLECTIONS ON LIFE AFTER LIFE** Dr. Raymond Moody	$1.95

Buy them at your local bookstore or use this handy coupon for ordering:

BOOKS BEHIND THE LINES:

The side of war you will never read about in the history books

Bantam Book Catalog

Here's your up-to-the-minute listing of every book currently available from Bantam.

This easy-to-use catalog is divided into categories and contains over 1400 titles by your favorite authors.

So don't delay—take advantage of this special opportunity to increase your reading pleasure.

Just send us your name and address and 25¢ (to help defray postage and handling costs).

BANTAM BOOKS, INC.
Dept. FC, 414 East Golf Road, Des Plaines, Ill. 60016

Mr./Mrs./Miss_____
(please print)

Address_____

City_____State_____Zip_____

Do you know someone who enjoys books? Just give us their names and addresses and we'll send them a catalog too!

_____

Mr./Mrs./Miss_____

Address_____

City_____State_____Zip_____

_____

Mr./Mrs./Miss_____

Address_____

City_____State_____Zip_____

FC—6/77